LOUIE:
AN OXFORD LADY

Doreen Louie West

ISIS
LARGE PRINT
Oxford and Orlando

First published in Great Britain 2000
by Nutty Books

Published in Large Print 2001 by ISIS Publishing Ltd,
7 Centremead, Osney Mead, Oxford OX2 0ES, and
ISIS Publishing, PO Box 195758,
Winter Springs, Florida 32719-5758, USA
by arrangement with Doreen Louie West

British Library Cataloguing in Publication Data
West, Doreen Louie, 1919-
    Louie: an Oxford lady. – Large print ed. – (ISIS
reminiscence series)
    1. Farm life – England – Oxfordshire 2. Large type books
    3. Oxfordshire (England) – Social life and customs
    I. Title
    942.5'7'083'092

ISBN 0-7531-9656-5 (hb)
ISBN 0-7531-9657-3 (pb)

Printed and bound by Antony Rowe, Chippenham and Reading

ACKNOWLEDGEMENT

I would like to thank my family and friends who have helped and encouraged me to write this book, especially Beryl, Val and Graham.

Doreen Louie West

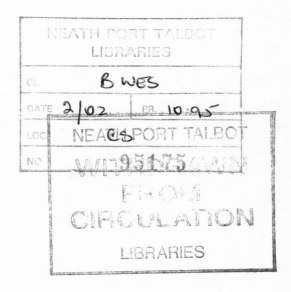

CHAPTER ONE

1943

Louie was writing at her kneehole desk in the bay window at the rear of her Oxford guest house and paused to gaze into the garden. The lawn needed cutting and she was sorely tempted to leave the mountains of paperwork and make the best of the sunny afternoon. She had received a telephone call that morning from a Mr Sloane enquiring if she had a double room vacant for him and his wife. He had made an appointment to view the room at five o'clock, so she would have time to spend a couple of hours tidying the garden before they arrived. Because of wartime food shortages most of the lawn in the back garden had been dug up to grow vegetables and beyond that was a wire pen where she kept her precious chickens.

Louie Hutt, now in her early fifties, was a farmer's daughter and wife and had brought up five children: Edwin, Doreen, Janet, Donald and Wilfred. She had separated from her husband, Algy, after he, in a fit of temper, forced her and the children to leave his farm. Her two teenage sons, Donald and Wilfred, were living with her, and Doreen, who had an eighteen month old daughter, Sylvia, was helping to run the guest house while her husband, Jack, was in the army.

Edwin, her eldest son, had been serving in the navy when his ship, the HMS *Cairo*, was torpedoed during the Malta Convoy Battle. He was rescued from the sea severely injured and died from his wounds in Gibraltar Hospital three months later. Janet was two years younger than Doreen and was now in the WAAF.

Algy had sold the family home, Mill Farm, Black Bourton, and had bought a smaller farm at Carswell, a village on the Oxford side of Faringdon. Home Farm consisted of a comfortable stone farmhouse with about ninety acres, plenty large enough for him and his housekeeper. He now regretted turning Louie and the children from their home, but Louie would not return.

At three minutes to five o'clock a large Humber saloon car pulled up outside Number Ten, Bradmore Road and a smart middle-aged gentleman stepped out of the driving seat and walked round to open the passenger door for a well dressed, plump lady in her late forties. Louie led Mildred and Henry Sloane to a spacious double bedroom on the first floor having shown them the lounge, dining room and bathroom which was shared with the other guests.

The gentleman smiled, "What a pleasant room. Do you like it, dear?"

His wife looked down her nose and proceeded to run her fingers round the furniture checking for dust. "Well, it's not what I'm used to, but I suppose it'll have to do."

"Do you know how long you'll be staying?" asked Louie, who was becoming irritated by the lady's unfortunate manner.

"I'm afraid I can't say," Henry Sloane replied. "It's just until we can find a house to rent. We've been living abroad but I shall now be working locally, so we are looking for a nice house where my wife can be near her sister who lives in Oxford."

After arranging to take the room in a week's time the couple left.

I hope they'll fit in with my other guests, thought Louie. Most of her boarders only stayed on a temporary basis but three: Bernard Jones, Olive Hasberry and Jane Worthing, seemed to have become permanent fixtures.

Bernard Jones, a rather smooth young man with a thin moustache, Brylcreemed hair and a slight limp, worked in Louie's local bank and was popular with the other guests. His friendly conversation and cheeky jokes led to a happy atmosphere as they all sat round the large dining table for their evening meal. Later they would gather in the comfortable lounge in sombre mood to listen to Louie's radio for the latest news from the war front.

Olive Hasberry, a good looking lady in her forties, was the manageress of an exclusive lady's dress shop in Oxford called La Mode and her tall, slim figure made the most of her fashionable outfits. She kept herself to herself and was out most evenings, Louie guessed that she was probably meeting a gentleman friend.

Jane Worthing was so shy that Louie was afraid she would never find a gentleman friend, although she confided in her, one day, that she thought Bernard Jones was very good looking and the image of Errol Flynn. A spinster in her late twenties, she dressed plainly and her hair was braided into two thin plaits which were pinned

3

in small bunches above her ears. She had a pretty face and with her bright eyes peering out through large spectacles, she reminded Louie of a timid little mouse. She worked in the accounts department of an Oxford book shop and had lost both her parents when she was in her teens. The highlight of her week was to visit her local cinema on a Saturday afternoon. She would return in the evening positively starry-eyed and liked to help Louie lay the dining table while she told her about the glamorous film stars she had seen or how frightened she had been watching the latest thriller. Louie was quite fond of Jane and, though she did not earn much money, she was never late paying her rent, gave everyone little gifts at Christmas and liked to help around the house.

Having spent most of her life on a farm Louie was used to providing plenty of good wholesome food for healthy appetites and when she married Algy she soon became renowned as the perfect hostess, preparing superb banquets for dinner guests and shooting parties. With wartime rationing, she was at her wits' end to provide acceptable meals from the plain, scant ingredients that were available. In fact, the arithmetic involved with coping with Ration Books etc. was her worst nightmare. Vera, the daughter of her friend, Simmy, worked at the Food Office and offered to help her with her paperwork, so, in desperation, Louie made an appointment to see her and set off into town.

Vera met her at the door and ushered her into her office.

"I thought it better that you come here," she said. "You seem to be in such a muddle it'll take some sorting out. If we're not careful you'll be claiming more rations than the Randolph Hotel." The Randolph was by far the largest and most prestigious hotel in Oxford. They both laughed but they knew that Louie could have been in serious trouble if she had claimed more rations than she was entitled to.

When Louie returned home Janet was waiting on the doorstep. She had been given a couple of day's leave, so hurried back to Bradmore Road to spend time with her family. She had just been promoted and was proudly wearing a propeller on her sleeve. She had spent her evenings studying for exams, the maths were particularly difficult for her, so she was very relieved to have passed. She was stationed at Newark servicing planes that were on operational flights. She told Doreen and Louie that the mechanics were often taken up for a trip, a cunning ploy to ensure that their work was not slack-twisted. Their hut was in a remote part of a potato field some distance from the ablutions and toilets, necessitating a perilous journey down a rough lane for which they were supplied with a bicycle. No one enjoyed the night time cycle rides, so the potatoes often benefited from an extra shower. The girls were advised not to get too involved with the air crews to avoid heartbreak if some of the planes did not return but this did not stop many a romance ending m tears.

Donald, on leaving school, had joined an electrical firm as an apprentice. He spent his days wiring army huts. He never complained and was determined to become an electrician, though he knew that it would not be long before he was conscripted for military service.

Wilfred had taken a job in a butcher's shop in the Covered Market in the centre of Oxford. He was a handsome lad and very popular with the housewives as he served them their meagre meat rations. An extra sausage or two, some tripe or half a pig's head to make some brawn were welcome additions. If you were a vegetarian you could have a small quantity of nuts instead. Babies and small children had a free bottle of concentrated orange juice and some rose hip syrup. Whole families would go out in the autumn gathering rose hips from the hedge-rows to sell for the production of the syrup. There was free milk for babies and all the school children had a small bottle, one third of a pint, for their elevenses.

St Hughes College had been turned into a military hospital and the matron had become friendly with Louie. The hospital was only a short walk from Louie's home in Bradmore Road. She often phoned to see if Louie could accommodate relatives when they came to visit patients, knowing that they would be comfortable there.

The telephone was ringing, Louie ran to answer it. This time it concerned the parents of a young soldier with a tumour on the brain.

"I need not tell you how serious it is Mrs Hutt, his mother and father are on their way from Coventry," Matron said. Louie was visualizing sleepless nights, but knew she could not refuse them. So often, Doreen and she had joined distraught relatives waiting all night for the telephone to ring, making endless cups of tea.

"I'll squeeze them in somewhere," she said.

She was glad she had not turned them away, Mr and Mrs Baker were a lovely couple. The next few days and nights were fraught with anxiety. Everyone at Number Ten was willing young Frank to pull through and thankfully he did. When he was well enough to leave hospital they brought him round to meet Louie before they travelled home. They stayed in touch for several years and Frank made a complete recovery.

The Sloanes arrived and, while Mildred rested in the lounge, Henry, Louie and Doreen man-handled several large trunks up the stairs to their room.

Henry joined the other guests for the evening meal, he seemed to get on well with them and it was not long before they were all on first name terms. He told Louie that Mildred had had such a tiring day that she had gone to bed early and wondered if she could have her supper in her room? Doreen arranged her meal daintily on a tray and took it up to her. She found Mildred sitting in the large double bed wearing a pink negligee, her face covered in cold cream.

"Thank you, dear," she said. "I might be able to manage just a morsel." However, when Doreen collected the tray later, there was not a scrap of food left.

The following morning Mildred did not come down to the dining room for her breakfast and Henry again asked if it could be taken to her room. Doreen dutifully obliged.

"Thank you so much," said Mildred, when Doreen returned for the tray. "I wonder if I could trouble you for some more toast and another cup of tea?"

Doreen smiled, "I'll see what I can do."

I'm soon going to have to put my foot down, she thought, *or this lady will have us running round after her all day*.

That evening, Mildred came down to dinner. From the kitchen, Louie and Doreen laughed as they heard her chattering to the other guests in a very loud voice, "Of course, this is not what I'm used to. Henry and I have been living in India and Singapore, where we had so many servants, I never had to lift a finger."

After dinner Mildred found the most comfortable arm chair in the lounge, plumped up the cushions and sat down. "Jane dear, I think I've left my reading glasses in my room. I wonder if you would be so kind as to fetch them for me?"

Jane scuttled out of the room and up the stairs, but returned empty handed looking worried, "I'm afraid I couldn't find them. I'm so sorry."

Mildred opened her handbag and peered in, "Oh silly me. They were here all the time."

Janet came home on weekend leave a month later and told them the good news that she would soon be posted to Locking Camp, near Weston-super-Mare. Their dear friend Edith, now married to her Jack, lived quite near and she would be able to visit them.

Louie thought it would be nice to take Janet to see a show while she was home, so she booked seats at the

Playhouse, a small Theatre in Oxford. She chose a matinée performance so that they could take Sylvia, who opted to sit on her Aunty Jan's lap. To Louie's relief she was on her best behaviour. The play had taken a serious turn, the lights went low and you could have heard a pin drop, when Sylvia suddenly sat up and called to her mother, who was sitting farther down the row.

"Mummy, my nicker lactic's too tight!" The drama turned into a comedy as you could hear the innocent remark all over the theatre. When they returned home Janet soon attended to the elastic and had a good tale to tell her friends when she returned to camp.

It was a glorious afternoon and Louie and Doreen had taken a little time off from their chores to relax in deck chairs in the garden while Sylvia played with her wooden horse. Louie was reading the *Oxford Times* in between cat naps.

"You don't often see a house to let these days. Here's one partly furnished with three reception rooms and six bedrooms. It's a box number."

"Shall I write for it?" asked Doreen after some thought. "I could take in paying guests while Jack is still in the army, but would you be able to manage all the work here?"

"I'm afraid you don't stand much chance, but no harm in trying and I'd manage somehow."

Two days later there was a ring at the front door and when Doreen opened it a very tall gentleman raised his hat.

"My name is Arthur Bellingham, I believe you replied to the advertisement regarding my house?"

"Please come in," said Doreen, quite taken aback.

"I've had sixty-five replies," he said, "but as you live so near I thought I'd give you first refusal. My house is just round the corner in Norham Road. I have to go abroad at short notice and need to find a tenant quickly. I'm asking four pounds a week rent. Would you be interested?"

"May my mother and I come and see the house?" said Doreen. "I'd have to have a word with my husband. It's a lot of money, but I think we could manage it."

It was a lovely old house, semi-detached with bay windows at the front and like so many Oxford houses in that area there was a basement. A long solid stone stairway led to the front door. "It used to belong to the Bishop of Oxford," said Mr Bellingham, "and he had so many children he enlarged the lounge and the bedroom above it to make a nursery."

"Did you like the house?" Louie asked Doreen that evening.

"Well, it's not what I'm used to," she joked, "but I suppose it'll have to do. Seriously though, I loved it. It might not be good enough for Mildred, but it would be good enough for me." She couldn't wait to telephone Jack, who sounded thrilled at the idea.

"I can't get home till next weekend," he said, "but you go ahead."

Everything went well and Jack decided to come straight home the following Friday night, so did not stop to change from his uniform. He was unable to get a pass to leave the camp that weekend but he took a chance and set out for Oxford on his lovely BMW motorcycle. He had not gone far however, when he was shocked to discover that the military police had set up a road block and were questioning drivers about their journey and how they had acquired their petrol. As he neared the blockade he was wondering how he was going to account for the fact that he did not have a pass when one of the policemen spotted his uniform.

"Are you a dispatch rider?" he shouted. Jack nodded. "Carry on then." He could not believe his luck as he revved-up the so obvious German machine and sped off. Had he been a dispatch rider his motorcycle, like all military vehicles, would have been sprayed with camouflage paint but it was pouring with rain and he guessed the lads wanted to return to camp as soon as possible.

Doreen took him round to see the house and they both agreed it was too good an opportunity to miss. They talked far into the night making plans and wondering how they were going to afford all the furniture they would need. Young couples were allotted coupons to buy Utility Furniture which was pretty basic but reasonably priced and would help to furnish the large empty rooms. They found bargains advertised in the *Oxford Mail* and in house sales and soon had everything ship-shape and Bristol fashion and were ready to move in, Doreen hopeful that they would soon find paying guests.

* * *

Simmy came most days to take Sylvia for walks in the nearby University Park. There was a duck pond at the far end and beyond, the river Cherwell separated the park from the meadows, both abounded with wild duck. Sylvia loved these walks and couldn't wait to get to the pond and feed the ducks. Simmy seemed just as enthusiastic. Doreen jokingly asked her, one day, if she was meeting a secret lover?

"Well not a lover, but I do meet several friends and there's one nice gentleman, a widower, who seems rather lonely and enjoys a chat. Don't tell your Jack, you know what a tease he is."

The first guests arrived, two ladies and a gentleman. They were working at a nearby college deciphering codes. Mrs James and Mrs Brenan both had husbands in the forces and Doreen noticed that they kept a watchful eye on their colleague, Mr Andersen, reminding him to take his medication and frequently checking on his whereabouts. He was Norwegian and very handsome but at times seemed preoccupied. The two ladies would come to the kitchen late at night to fill their hot water bottles and have a chat, so, one evening, she asked them if Mr Andersen was unwell as he took so many pills.

They told her that he was slowly coming to terms with a very traumatic experience that he had had whilst serving in the Norwegian Resistance Movement. He and several comrades were allotted the task of blowing up a bridge that carried a train load of ammunition. Afterwards, they were to congregate in a small bay where they would be picked up by a British vessel and taken to England. Everything went according to plan and they waited on the beach. There was no sign of the vessel or the small boat to row them out to it. They waited for what seemed an eternity when his best friend, who was at the end of his tether, went berserk. The leader had to make a decision, they drew lots and it fell to Mr Andersen to pull the trigger to silence his friend, or else it would have been certain death for all of them. They waited another hour knowing there was no way out of the cove and wondering if the Germans had heard the shot. It was a dark night and it was not until they heard the plopping of oars on the water and the sound of English voices that they breathed again and waded into the sea carrying their dead comrade to the boat.

"Mr Andersen is a very talented man," said Mrs James. "He speaks many languages, and is invaluable at the college. He works so hard, maybe that helps him to forget."

After he had been staying a while he liked to join Doreen and Jack for a quiet chat. He told them about his family and how much he was missing his lovely home in Norway. He described the beautiful countryside and said that in winter the best way to get around was on skis, it was a way of life even for young children. He invited them to stay with him after the war. Coded messages had got through to him to say that his wife and children were safe, but they dare not write to each other.

"I'm sure this war can't last much longer," said Doreen. "There are rumours that the Americans are coming to our aid."

Little did she realize how close the rumours were to reality. The next morning Louie telephoned Doreen to say that she had been contacted regarding accommodation for some American Army officers.

"I told them I could take two," she said, "but I've only got one room to spare so they'll have to share."

The next day the college telephoned Doreen to ask if she had room for yet another of their staff.

"Well, I have got a room," she was going to say that it was rather small, but the lady interrupted her.

"Great! I'll send him along." So that was that.

The door bell rang an hour later and Doreen opened the door to behold the tallest, most handsome man she had ever seen, dressed in American naval officer's uniform, with a most disarming smile.

"Mrs West?" he enquired. She nodded, too taken aback to speak. He held out his hand. "I'm George Holt. I understand you have a room for me." Doreen's heart sank, she had managed to save enough coupons to buy a Utility bed but it was none too comfortable and smaller than average and she wondered how in the world this giant of a man was going to squeeze into it. When she showed him the room he just said, "This will suit me fine. Some days I have to stay in and rest as I suffer from asthma, I hope you won't mind?"

"I'm well used to that," Doreen told him. "My brother suffered from it." She could picture his discomfort, crammed in that bed for long periods and resolved to do something about it. However, events took a turn when he came into the kitchen one evening. Doreen looked up from her ironing.

"I've brought my fiancée to meet you. Doreen meet Dorina." Dorina was a naval officer, so small and neat in her smart uniform. "We've known each other for some time now and have decided to get married tomorrow. We see no point in waiting. Is it all right if Dorina moves in with me?"

Doreen liked her from the start, "Of course she can."

"And could we have a double bed?" Three minds, but a single thought, *that Utility bed*, and they all burst out laughing. Doreen produced a small bottle of Whiskey that she had been hoarding for Christmas and they sat chatting till midnight. They told her that George had two adorable children, living in the States, but was divorced from his wife. His father was a great friend of President Roosevelt. Dorina had been married to a naval officer who was killed while they were stationed on Malta. On her return to England she joined the WRENS, met George, and they fell in love.

They were wed at the Registry Office, both in their uniforms, he so tall and she so petite. They came back to the hurriedly arranged reception in Doreen's lounge. She had made a cake that morning but, as rations did not run to icing sugar, she made a small horseshoe out of silver paper for decoration and tied a ribbon round it. The guests toasted the happy couple with some of Louie's home-made elderberry wine.

George had lived in Woodstock, Connecticut and was very keen to visit Woodstock, Oxfordshire, so they spent their short honeymoon at a hotel there. When they returned, the double bed had arrived!

CHAPTER
TWO

Jack came home the next weekend, he was very unhappy in the army as he had never had to take orders since leaving school. He had made his own way in the world, so consequently the discipline was extra hard for him, though his skills as a mechanic soon earned him a stripe on his arm and in a very short time he was promoted to sergeant.

"I think I'll soon be posted to Bicester," he told Doreen. He was to be put in charge of a workshop repairing army lorries.

"I'll be able to get home every night to be with my girls," he said, giving Sylvia a hug.

"I'm sure I can find you some washing-up to do," said Doreen.

"Anything would be preferable to being at camp. I think I'll get the cars out of storage. If I can save up enough petrol coupons we might manage a few short trips. Perhaps we could take Louie for a ride out now and again, I'm sure she needs a break." When he was called up, he had stored two of his cars: a Jaguar and an Austin Seven, in a farmer's barn. Not only was petrol in short supply, but tyres were a precious commodity because 90% of the world's natural rubber resources were in enemy hands. The Ministry of Supply placed regular advertisements in the newspapers asking people to "Go easy with your tyres" and giving advice as to how to conserve them. Even the Oxford Bus Services had had to be restricted leading to considerable overcrowding for passengers trying to get to and from work.

"It seems ages since we've all had a ride out together in the car, it would be lovely," replied Doreen, "even if only as far as The Trout for a drink. What a treat that would be!" The Trout was a charming country inn on the banks of the river Thames just outside Oxford, in a hamlet called Godstow. It was a very popular hostelry where, on warm summer evenings, one could sit outside on the terrace, watch the trout rising in the fast running water and listen to the eerie calls of peacocks.

George and Dorina had bought two bicycles and took great pleasure in cycling around the countryside. They especially loved going to Woodstock.

Dorina liked to come down to the kitchen and chat while Doreen was cooking the evening meal. "I think George misses his children more than he lets on," she said. "We'd like to have a child, but I'm thirty five, I hope I'm not too old?"

Now that Jack was stationed at Bicester and came home at night, the large comfortable kitchen was a real home from home in the evenings. Doreen's brothers, Don and Wilf, were crazy about motorcycles and chattered endlessly to Jack on their favourite subject. He had owned and ridden motorcycles since he was fourteen and was determined to ride in the TT races in the Isle of Man when the war ended.

Louie would sometimes join them, but like Doreen, she was busy running her guest house, so they did most of their chatting on the telephone.

"How are you getting on with your American lads?" asked Doreen, one day, "and what about Mildred, is she still as demanding?"

"I'm finding the lads rather difficult, they don't talk very much. I get the impression that they resent being here, but perhaps I'm wrong. I expect they're worried about what lies ahead," said Louie. "Mildred's not so bad. Henry's at work all day, so she gets up late in the morning and goes out shopping or visiting her sister. He often takes her out in the evenings to the theatre or concerts. She buys so many expensive new clothes, I don't know how she gets enough clothing coupons. Olive told me that she visited La Mode the other day and tried on two or three dresses that were a size too small for her. She then left saying that they lacked the quality she was looking for. The other guests have got wise to her now and even Jane finds excuses not to run her errands. Henry has taken her to see several houses, but none are good enough. I suspect she doesn't want the work of running her own home."

"I wonder what Henry does for a living? He must earn plenty of money to keep up with Mildred's expensive tastes," said Doreen.

"He's never said what he does and I don't like to ask, but he speaks several languages fluently, perhaps he's an interpreter. He's such a nice man, so polite, kind and friendly in a quiet sort of way."

"It sounds as if you're quite smitten, Mother," laughed Doreen.

"Oh no!" Louie was quick to respond. "To me, he's just another guest, though I think Mildred is very lucky to have such a thoughtful husband."

When Louie had any spare time her great joy was to take Sylvia on an outing. They would sometimes go on a bus to Summertown to visit Oliver and Gurdens, a factory famous for its delicious cakes. Everyone was allowed two shillings and sixpence worth and a queue would form the length of two streets when the aroma of cakes baking drifted around the neighbourhood. They would wait patiently in the queue till Sylvia could choose her favourite date tarts which were covered in thick chocolate.

She was taking her for a walk in the parks one Sunday afternoon, when she spotted Henry in the distance sitting on a bench near the river, just gazing into the water. She knew that Mildred was at home having an afternoon nap, so he was obviously enjoying the peace and quiet. She took hold of Sylvia's hand and hurried her away, not wanting to disturb him.

One evening Jack bought a large wooden rocking horse from a friend whose children had outgrown it. He had some funny looks as he carried it through Oxford in the semi-darkness and his arms were aching by the time he reached Norham Road, but the joy on Sylvia's face the following morning when she had her first ride on it, more than compensated.

"It's my very bestest toy, Granny," she told Louie.

Jack brought his two cars home, washed off the layers of dust and after a good polish they stood proudly in the driveway. He decided, one day, to use some of his precious petrol coupons and drive to the camp in the Jaguar. The commanding officer came into the yard as he was parking it. Jack gave a salute and noted the admiration on his face.

"That's a very nice car you have, West. Is it yours?"

"Yes sir," Jack replied and walked towards the workshop. The officer followed him.

"I don't suppose you would consider lending it to me occasionally? I had a Jaguar but had to get rid of it when war broke out." Jack was silent. "I would see you right for petrol."

"All right then," Jack agreed, "but only if I'm not using it." He gave a cheeky grin, secretly delighted to have found a fellow Jaguar fan and also an extra source of petrol.

Colonel King would often come into the workshop to discuss the merits of his favourite car. Whenever he borrowed it, it was always returned with a full tank of petrol and spotlessly clean. Jack thought that he must have spent as much time polishing as driving even though he had clocked up quite a few miles.

Jack had promised to take George, Dorina and Louie for a ride and Doreen was making cakes, ready for the picnic. Jack had just come home and was playing with Sylvia in the garden, when the telephone rang. Doreen answered it.

"It's Colonel King, he wants to borrow the Jag," she told Jack, unable to hide her disappointment. "He wants to visit his family in Northampton tomorrow and take them out for a drive." She felt sure that was the end of their promised picnic.

"Tell him I can't let him have the Jag, he can have the Austin Seven."

"I think he'll be a bit disappointed," said Doreen, she could picture the Colonel and his family crammed into the little Austin while the Sergeant and his family rode in style in the Jaguar. Jack stood his ground and Doreen was apprehensive as she returned to the phone to deliver his message. The Colonel was obviously not pleased but he agreed to borrow the little car. She went into the garden and gave her husband a hug.

"I didn't want to disappoint my girls, but most of all, I'm not missing those jam buns," he said, picking Sylvia up to carry her indoors, shoulder high.

The Colonel came to collect the Austin early the next morning, in high spirits, and said he was looking forward to seeing his family. When he returned in the evening, he told Jack that he'd had a most enjoyable time. "Topping little car! West," he said. "My grandchildren thought it was great fun. I must admit though, I still prefer the Jaguar. We had to negotiate a steep hill and I was afraid we might have to get out and push, but it chugged to the top, with the children laughing all the way."

"Well," said Jack, "I'll make sure you have the Jag next time, Sir."

* * *

The weather that summer was lovely, Doreen invited their friends, Edith and Jack, for a fortnight's holiday. They decided to nickname Edith's Jack: "Jacky", to distinguish between the two friends. Janet managed to get a week's leave to spend with them. Jacky loved children and wherever he was, Sylvia was not far away. Many happy hours were spent in the park. Edith and Janet would sit and talk while Jacky and Sylvia played with a ball or went to the river to watch the ducks. He delighted in Sylvia's infectious laughter as she watched them performing strange antics as they searched underwater for titbits, sometimes only their tales protruding from the water. Edith's great hobby was knitting and wherever she went you could hear her needles clicking, all her friends proudly wearing their new cardigans, hats and gloves.

The Colonel had borrowed the Jaguar the previous weekend. As always, he had left a full tank of petrol and the car shone like a new pin, so Jack planned an outing for the Saturday. Doreen packed a picnic lunch and they made an early start. Sylvia never enjoyed motoring, she suffered dreadfully from car sickness, so it was decided they would not go far.

"Just a little mystery tour," said Jack as he donned a chauffeur's cap that he kept for fooling around, and off they went.

First it was to the camp to show them where he worked. The soldier on the gate recognized the car as they approached and gave Jack a cheeky salute to everyone's amusement.

22

Then it was off to Oxford, over Carfax and down St Aldates to where the River Thames runs under Folly Bridge.

"We thought a river trip on one of Salter's Steamers might be fun," said Doreen, this met with everyone's approval. They were soon aboard, sitting on deck in the warm sunshine, picnic baskets at the ready, so much to see and talk about. By the time they reached Wallingford the baskets were empty, so a meal at a riverside hotel was the order of the day. The early start and fresh air had given them a healthy appetite and they did justice to the good plain wartime fare, topped off with roly-poly pudding and custard. Jack told them he liked custard so much when he was a small boy that he used to eat it with a fork to make it last longer. The sun was setting when they returned to the mooring.

As they drove home over Carfax Doreen spotted Jimmy Dingle, a famous Oxford character, who dressed in top hat and tails and carried a sandwich-board. Tonight it advertised a Variety Show at the New Theatre. Topping the bill was "Big-Hearted Arthur Askey", Jacky's favourite comedian, so a trip to the theatre was hastily arranged.

Louie was weeding in her vegetable patch, one afternoon, bending over to snatch the weeds from under the beans. *Why do the weeds always grow faster than the veg?* she thought. She felt a gentle tap on her shoulder and nearly jumped out of her skin. She looked up to see Henry Sloane smiling down at her.

"I'm so sorry. I didn't mean to startle you," he said. "I've got the afternoon off and wondered if you'd like a hand in the garden?"

Louie was taken aback, "It's very kind of you to offer, but I wouldn't want to trouble you."

"I used to love gardening when we lived in Dorset. Nothing would give me greater pleasure, and I could do with the exercise."

They spent a pleasant hour weeding and hoeing before Mildred came home and it was time for Louie to prepare the evening meal. She had enjoyed Henry's company, he seemed so happy and relaxed.

After that, he became quite a regular helper in the garden. He always seemed to know just what wanted doing; he didn't mind the dirty jobs and even offered to creosote the chicken house.

Louie and Henry found so much to talk about while they worked, they had similar interests, Henry having been brought up on a farm in Dorset. He told Louie about his work abroad.

He was a civil servant working for the Foreign Office and had been stationed abroad for the last fifteen years, mostly in Singapore and India. Luckily, they had left Singapore some time before the Japanese invasion. He specialized in linguistics and was now back in England to work in an advisory capacity.

His post abroad had enabled him and his wife to live in luxury, a substantial house and servants were allocated with the job. He longed to return home to the English way of life, though he knew that Mildred did not have the same feelings, she had been in her element in the lavish lifestyle. Louie found it easy to confide in Henry about her marriage and life with Algy, and told him things that she could never bring herself to discuss with anyone else.

* * *

Mr Andersen, Mrs James and Mrs Brenan found a small house to rent and decided to share, so when the American Airforce base at Heyford needed accommodation for some officers, Doreen agreed to take four.

"I think you're being a bit chancy," said Louie, "but you may have better luck than me."

The two lieutenants were first to arrive, they were charming young men. Their uniforms so much smarter than the British officers, Doreen could well understand why the girls found them so attractive. A coach picked them up in the morning at six o'clock and brought them home in time for their evening meal. They said they would not need breakfast as they could get it in camp. When they returned in the evening they would come clattering down the stairs to the basement kitchen to say "Hi" and take Sylvia up to their rooms for cookies. Many parcels were sent to them from home. One of the lads was in charge of the catering and would sometimes bring some tins of dried eggs, spam or tinned fruit, which was gratefully received. He assured Doreen that he had been given permission to dispose of the damaged tins.

Next to arrive was Captain Wright, he was older than the other officers and Doreen learned that he was an eye specialist.

Last of the four was a very young Major Gillingham. Doreen wondered how he had attained his rank so early in life, but decided his charm must have had something to do with it. She was sure she had the pick of the

American forces, they even insisted on making their beds in the morning though she had told them not to bother. Major Gillingham shared Jack's love of motorcycles and, after lengthy discussions concerning clutches and carburettors, a short ride round the back roads on Jack's BMW made his day.

Jack had heard that a farmer from Bletchingdon, a village not far from Oxford, was selling duck eggs, so he suggested they take Louie out for a ride one Sunday. Sylvia was in her element, everywhere she looked there were ducks all shapes and sizes. The farmer said it would be a good idea to buy a couple to rear and fatten for Christmas.

"If there be a fair few of you, I'd have Muscovies, they're a bit bigger," he said.

Doreen said that there would be a fair few as Dorina, George and the Americans would not be going home for Christmas. Quick as a flash he caught a duck and drake and popped them into a cardboard box.

"Can you manage to kill them, Jack?" asked Louie on the homeward journey.

"I couldn't kill a fly," said Jack. "No way! Doreen was brought up on a farm, she can do it." Doreen did not answer. She had killed and dressed chickens from the age of ten, but Algy, her father, had always killed the ducks. Watching the concerned expression on Sylvia's face she knew that Dilly and Billy had come to Norham Road to stay. They were to live in the garden protected from predators by a high brick wall and an old summer-house provided night-time comfort. Christmas came and went and they were still ruling the roost in the West's household and pecking the kitchen window at tea-time demanding to be fed.

Dorina came down to the kitchen one evening, with George in close pursuit. Doreen guessed they had good news by the delighted look on their faces.

"I am so pleased for you," she said hugging them both, but she knew she would soon be losing her favourite guests as they would be needing a home with a nursery.

Dorina and George had moved into their house leaving just the Americans, so Doreen decided to paint the bathroom and toilet. The label on the paint tin read "Quick Drying", therefore she reasoned that if she painted the toilet first it would be dry by evening. Soon the little room, toilet seat and all, was gleaming in bright green paint and she set about the bathroom, hoping to finish in time to prepare the evening meal. By then, she hoped the paint would at least be feeling tacky, but to her horror it was as wet as when she put it on.

She telephoned her mother, "Whatever can I do? They'll be home soon."

"I'll come over," said Louie in fits of laughter imagining the consequences, *and bright green too!*

Louie was soon on the doorstep, armed with a large bottle of turpentine and a bundle of rags, she headed for the stairs. They rubbed and scrubbed and soon the smartly painted toilet seat was back to square one.

"I wonder how long I'll have to leave these up?" Doreen sighed as she wrote WET PAINT notices in bold letters.

A very long time, Louie thought, and suggested a cup of tea. As they sat round the kitchen table with Sylvia chattering non-stop to her Granny, Louie noticed dabs of green paint in her golden curls and on her frock.

"I had a letter from your father this morning," she told Doreen. "He wants me to go back to him. He sent a photo of the house and says I would like it there."

Doreen was apprehensive, she hoped her mother would not risk another temper tantrum. "Are you going?"

"No." Louie got up from the table. "I must go and start cooking the evening meal. You'd better keep the turpentine, you may need it." She kissed them both and hurried off.

"OPEN THE SECOND FRONT NOW" was daubed on every available wall space all over Britain. Doreen wondered who was responsible, obviously not the lads in the armed forces or their families. She never mentioned it to Jack, but dreaded the implications knowing it would not be long. She was thankful that Don and Wilf were not old enough to be conscripted, but her lovely American boys would surely be involved.

Doreen's guests were soon joined by two Polish airmen. They had escaped from Poland and were experienced pilots, she had no doubt their skills would be needed when the push came. They spoke perfect English and, like the Americans, were charming lads.

When Captain Wright was posted his room was taken by a young lady, Miss Musselmans. She was employed as a driver for the American officers. Her uniform, which included trousers, concealed her withered legs, the result of suffering polio when she was a child. None the less, she drove the large limousines with great skill. Her father had come from Holland at the beginning of the war and moved to Rousham House, a lovely mansion not far from Oxford, to accommodate his large family of ten children. He was very proud of his plucky daughter doing her bit for the war effort in spite of her handicap. Every week the family nanny came to massage her poor legs and would call on Doreen for a chat and a cup of tea, updating her on the latest news from Rousham House. Her great concern was for the fabulous furniture which was taking quite a battering at the hands of so many boisterous children. Mrs Musselmans often sent a rabbit or bunch of daffodils from the estate which was gratefully received.

It was the first week in December and Olive asked Louie if she would have room for an extra guest over Christmas. She had received a distressing letter from a friend, Doris Chambers, who lived in Torcross near Slapton in Devon. A large area of land around Slapton Sands, 30,000 acres, was to be requisitioned by the War Office and this included Torcross and several other villages. All the occupants were to be evacuated by 20 December as the land was needed for troop-training. They had been told not to expect to return to their homes for at least six months. Doris, who was retired, was devastated. She lived in a charming cottage with her little dog and budgerigar and wondered what state it would be in when she was allowed to return. She was going to stay with relatives in Norfolk, but was anxious not to impose on them for too long.

Louie said that of course she would be welcome to stay.

"What about her dog and budgerigar?" asked Olive. "I know you don't usually encourage guests to bring their pets."

"They'll be welcome too, as long as the dog doesn't chase my chickens," Louie laughed.

CHAPTER
THREE

Not long after Doris had moved in with Louie, Major Gillingham told Doreen that he and his three colleagues would be confined to barracks for a few days and would be taking their belongings. She guessed something was afoot.

Janet, who had been coming home on leave, telephoned to say that leave was cancelled. Doreen did not sleep that night wondering if Jack would be going and how soon? He had been working all the hours God sends for weeks preparing lorries and some nights had not managed to get home.

The next day the Polish pilots reluctantly said their farewells and only Miss Musselmans was left. The house felt very empty and Doreen telephoned her mother to tell her about the sudden exodus. Louie's two American lads had gone too.

Doreen wondered if she would be able to find guests to fill the empty rooms but need not have worried, a young doctor from the Radcliffe Infirmary soon took up residence, his name was Doctor Cane.

Louie had a new guest, Mrs Slesenger, who was the wife of an American politician. "She's very nice, but rather grand," laughed Louie. "She arrived in a limousine and later a van load of luggage was delivered. She's even brought her own bed. Perhaps she's heard about our Utility furniture. Mildred was very impressed."

Despite the tense situation on the war front, Louie was determined to provide a good Christmas for her guests. Wilf was the proud provider of a goose together with other oddments that he had earned through working overtime at the butcher's shop. Don managed to shoot a couple of rabbits which Louie cooked in a delicious rabbit pie for Boxing Day. Doris Chambers had settled in well and all the guests were in cheery mood. Even Mildred entered into the party spirit after a few glasses of home-made wine.

In spite of the atrocious weather the big day had arrived. On D-day 6 June, British and allied forces landed on Utah Beach to continue the struggle to free the world of the threat of German domination. Doreen worried constantly about the lads battling their way for supremacy on the shores of France and hoped against hope that her new found friends would come through unscathed.

It was during this harrowing time that good news arrived. A very excited George telephoned to say that Dorina had given birth to a baby boy and all was well.

Doreen was feeling very low, she had found a lump in her neck. She put off seeing her Doctor, but it was growing bigger so she finally made up her mind to do something about it. She had not told Louie or Jack hoping it would go away. When she mentioned it to Dr Cane he advised her to visit her GP as soon as possible and hinted that an operation may be necessary. His advice later proved to be correct. Doreen was given an appointment to see a specialist who prescribed Ultra-Violet Ray treatment, hoping to avoid an operation. Doreen had treatment twice a week which involved standing in front of a lamp with an open flickering flame. This seemed to have an adverse effect and as the weeks went by the wretched lump seemed to thrive, getting larger and more painful. Doreen mentioned it to the nurse.

"That's all right," she replied. "It has to get bigger before it gets better."

By the time she saw the specialist again, her neck was not a pretty sight.

"Why haven't you been back before?" he said. "This was obviously the wrong treatment." Doreen, not wanting to get the nurse into trouble, did not answer. "You'll have to come in for an operation." Her heart sank though she knew it would come to this and she wondered how she was going to be able to leave Sylvia and all her guests?

Jack said he could get compassionate leave to look after Sylvia. The guests, who were very understanding, found temporary accommodation. The weeks went by and no word from the hospital. Doreen was worried about the rent, she could not afford to pay four pounds a week out of her thirty five shillings army allowance and did not like to bother Jack, so decided to go to the hospital to see if they might give her a definite date for her admittance. The girl at the Appointments Desk glanced through some papers and said abruptly that there was nothing she could do.

"You'll have to wait till you hear from us."

Doreen, near to tears, headed for the door and nearly bumped into a young man in a white coat, it was Dr Cane.

"What are you doing here?" he said, taking her hand. "I was hoping to hear from you to say that I could come back home."

Doreen explained her predicament.

"Wait here," he said and headed towards the Appointments Desk. In minutes he came back. "How soon would you be able to come in? What about tomorrow?"

So tomorrow it was! Louie would often say: "It's not always *what* you know, it's *who* you know that counts." Doreen was so relieved, but did not want to jump the queue, the good Doctor assured her this was not the case.

Whilst in hospital Doreen met Mrs Prior, a farmer's wife, who was in the same ward. She lived in the lovely village of Filkins, just a few miles from Black Bourton where Doreen lived as a girl. They became great friends so the Sister had their beds moved next to each other. Mrs Prior's husband, George, came to visit as often as he could but running a farm and a milk round left him little spare time. He brought strawberries from his garden and cream from his dairy herd, which he insisted Doreen share with them. Mrs Prior was about Louie's age and when she visited they struck up a friendship which was to last a lifetime, they had so much in common. Mrs Prior had been Nanny to the children of a wealthy family, the Goodenoughs, who lived in a large imposing house in Filkins. She had had a nursery maid to help her and used to make beautiful clothes for the children, whom she adored. Sadly, when she met and married George they were not blessed with any children of their own.

The lump in Doreen's neck was caused by a TB gland. The operation took longer than expected as other glands had been affected, so it was a fortnight before she was allowed home. All her immediate family had to be tested for any signs of TB but thankfully all the results were clear.

George Prior telephoned to say that his wife was home from hospital and invited them all to tea the next day. They were so looking forward to meeting Sylvia as children were not allowed to visit in hospital.

"I won't be able to go," said Jack. "Would you like to take the Jag, if you feel up to driving?"

"Yes please," said Doreen enthusiastically. "I'm sure I could manage that!"

It was a lovely day and Doreen, Louie and Sylvia set off for Filkins in fine style. When they arrived George was busy milking. Sylvia was fascinated, she had never been so near to a cow before. She stood watching as the milk squirted into the pail.

The farmhouse was typically Cotswold, built of stone with mullion windows. Its garden, which was surrounded by a dry stone wall, abounded with colour. They sat on a wooden seat in the sunshine and talked until George had finished his chores, then went indoors for a farmhouse tea with lashings of cream and butter for the home-made scones. With butter rationed to two ounces a week this was much appreciated. Mrs Prior poured the tea into fine china cups, with an outsize mug for George.

"Would you rather have milk, Sylvia?" she asked.

Sylvia hesitated for a moment. "No thank you Mrs Prior, I only like milk out of a bottle." The idea of it being squeezed out of a cow obviously did not appeal, which highly amused George. After tea he took them for a walk round the farm, first to the pig sties to see the pigs.

"You'd better not tell Sylvia where bacon comes from," he said when she was out of earshot.

"I don't know when I enjoyed myself so much," said Louie as they were driving back to Oxford. Doreen wondered if a taste of the country would change her mind about returning to Algy, but it did not.

That evening, as her guests were talking round the dinner table, Louie could hear Mildred's voice rise above the others as she turned to Mrs Slesenger. "We do so enjoy going to the theatre. This week we went to The Playhouse and saw a comedy by Noel Coward called: 'Tonight at 8.30'. It was so amusing. It's quite a pleasant little theatre and you meet such a nice class of person there. You must come with us one day, Henry always reserves the best seats."

Bernard Jones could not resist the temptation to respond to Mildred's remarks. "It sounds quite nice doesn't it Jane? Why don't we go one evening?"

36

"Bernard, you're always teasing me," Jane blushed. "It's a good thing I don't take you seriously."

"I'm not teasing," said Bernard with a mischievous grin. "I'll reserve a couple of seats and we'll go next week if there's a decent play on. That's if you'd like to go?"

Louie hoped that Bernard had not raised Jane's hopes only to let her down. She had seen him flirting with some of the young girls at the bank where he worked and did not think Jane was his type. He did not seem to have a steady girl friend and when he moved into the guest house she had asked him if he was married. "Not me," he replied. "I'm as free as a bird." But Louie remained unconvinced.

Two days later, Bernard placed two Playhouse Theatre tickets on the mantelpiece for all to see. They were for good seats, having cost two shillings and sixpence each, for an evening performance of a comedy drama called "Strange Orchestra" and booked for the following Thursday.

"There you are Jane," he said. "Just to prove I'm not teasing."

Jane was overcome. "It would be lovely, but I must pay for my ticket."

"No, it's my treat. Time you had a bit of fun."

Jane spent the next few days in a nervous state of anticipation. Mrs Slesenger noticed that she was becoming increasingly anxious and took Louie to one side. "Do you think Jane would be offended if I offered to lend her something to wear? I reckon we're about the same size."

"I'm sure she would be pleased, after all, there is a war on, we all have to be economical with our clothing coupons," said Louie.

Mrs Slesenger took Jane to her room and found a smart suit that fitted her perfectly, together with a jaunty little hat. "Wow Jane, you'll knock 'em dead!" she exclaimed, pleased with her handiwork.

The big day came and Jane was ready in plenty of time. "I mustn't keep Bernard waiting."

Bernard's eyes lit up when he saw her, "You look smashing! What a great honour it will be to escort you, Madam."

When they returned, it was quite late and Louie was in the kitchen making a hot drink. She heard a little tap on the door.

"May I come in?" said Jane. "I just had to tell you what a wonderful time I've had. It was a bit posh in the theatre, but everyone was ever so nice. I enjoyed the play and the acting was very clever. Bernard was such a gentleman, he bought me a programme and made me feel really special. I shall never forget tonight as long as I live."

Louie was so relieved that Bernard had not let her down. After that, he would sometimes accompany her to the cinema, he seemed to genuinely enjoy her company. "We've had a laugh haven't we, Jane?" he would say. "Just a bit of fun." Louie did not think he ever intended to become romantically involved. She hoped that Jane, who seemed so happy and self-assured, had not fallen in love with him.

* * *

Our gallant fighting forces and their allies were battling their way through France and still Jack worked to prepare supply lorries to be sent to the front.

Doreen's guests had returned and they were joined by Mr Stanford, an architect who had been invalided out of the army. He had been stationed somewhere near the Himalayas and told her fascinating stories about the way people lived in that part of the World.

CHAPTER
FOUR

A yard with a row of lock-up garages came up for rent in Denmark Street and Jack's friend, Alfie Plaisted, thought it would be a good idea for Jack to start a business there.

"I could help you," he said. "We could buy and sell a few cars and motorcycles and do repairs. Then you'll be set up for when you come out of the army."

"What time do you think I've got?" said Jack, but he let himself be talked into it and was accepted as a tenant.

Alfie, who weighed around twenty stone, was a great character, it was quite amazing that a man of his size could work so hard and be so full of life. He was always first in the queue for a newspaper at the *Oxford Times* Office and if there was a car advertised, which was a rare occurrence, he would be first on the vendor's doorstep to try to bring off a deal. He was married with two daughters of whom he was justly proud.

If Louie or Doreen needed furniture, he was the man to find it.

Many of Jack's friends had joined the Oxford and Bucks Light Infantry because they were told they would not have to go overseas. Within a short time many were posted abroad, some to Japan, only to be taken prisoner and only a few survived.

The Germans were losing their stronghold in Europe and it looked as if the war with Germany would soon be over. When, at last, peace was declared, it was like having a huge weight lifted from your shoulders. Our brave servicemen and women were victorious, but at what cost? News of losses and casualties seemed to take forever to filter through. An excited Dorina telephoned Doreen to say that George was safe and on his way home to America, she was leaving the next day with baby John to join him. However, Louie and Doreen heard no more of their other American and Polish guests and often wondered what became of them.

Olive received a long letter from Doris, who had returned to her cottage in Torcross. She was relieved to find that no actual damage had occurred to her home, but it was in a sad state of neglect and the garden was a wilderness. Other people in the area had not been so lucky, their properties had been badly damaged and although compensation had been promised they held out little hope that it would cover all their losses. The training exercise that had taken place must have been vast judging by the acreage that was laid waste and it was obvious that many troops had taken part. The whole exercise had been such a closely guarded secret that it was very difficult for the local people to find out what had happened. There was speculation that US troops were involved, also rumours of bodies found floating in the sea and mass graves. None of these tales had been substantiated and it would take a long time for Doris and her neighbours, especially the farmers, to put the area to rights, she doubted whether it would ever feel the same again.

A few months later Janet's unit in the WAAF was disbanded but she soon found a job as a receptionist in a hotel, The Catherine Wheel, in Henley on Thames.

Now that the war was over Doreen was finding pleasure in the most simple things: not having to pull the blackout curtains and to be able to walk out at night with a torch. Her happiness was marred when she received a distressing letter from her friend, Margery. Margery had lived with Doreen and Janet in their land army days and was now married to a top jockey, Mickey Greening. They had a little boy, Richard, and lived in Newmarket. While playing in the stable yard the little lad had fallen backwards into a bucket of boiling water and was so badly scalded that they were not allowed to see him for weeks. Happily, he was now well on the road to recovery. Doreen was thrilled when Margery telephoned her to say that Mick would be away at a race meeting and could she bring Richard up to Oxford for a few days?

The two children got on famously, Louie enjoyed seeing Margery and her lovely little boy again and joined them all in the evenings. Doreen suggested they go to the Cinema as there was a good film on at the Regal. Janet managed to get the afternoon off so, armed with a bag of boiled sweets, not daring to take toffees for fear of rustling the papers and upsetting people in the audience, they set off. The Newsreel came before the main film and included the result of the day's big horse race.

Suddenly a little voice exclaimed, "That's my Dad and he's winning. Come on Dad!" He stood up in his excitement. "He's won Mummy!" as the leading horse flew past the winning post.

A lady lent forward from the row behind. "Was it really his Dad?" Margery nodded and the immediate audience clapped.

The next day Margery had news that her sister, Babs, who was in the ATS, was soon to be demobbed and would be looking for a job. She had been a driver, but with so many service men and women coming home, jobs were few and far between.

"Do you think she'd like to work in a hotel?" Janet asked Margery.

"Beggars can't be choosers, I think she'll be pleased to get any job. Why, have you anything in mind?"

"I may have." Janet would not be drawn, but said she would let her know. Before the end of the week Babs had had an interview and was happily working at The Catherine Wheel.

Henley on Thames was exceptionally beautiful that year, the rhododendrons in the surrounding woods had excelled themselves and the girls took long walks in the afternoons and brought back some bunches to decorate the hotel. Janet arranged a snack bar with dainty tempting titbits, a new innovation to the main restaurant, which became very popular.

* * *

Donald had finished his apprenticeship and was now a qualified electrician, but decided to take a job with a motorcycle firm. He thought his electrical skills would be an asset and like so many lads of his age was crazy about motorcycles. He was keen to learn the mechanics, but keener still to ride them out on test drives. On one such occasion he was happily riding a machine up the Banbury Road, travelling at considerably more miles per hour than was permitted in a built up area and quite oblivious to the fact that he was being followed by a police car. It was early in the morning so there was little traffic, but this did not cut any ice with the constable, resulting in poor Don losing his licence and being confined to the workshop.

The motorcycle shop was near The Oxpens in Oxford which was used as a cattle market, but when not in use, was quite deserted. Having completed work on a motorcycle and sidecar one morning, the temptation was too great, *surely a little spin would be all right?*

Don kicked up the machine and started off, he had never ridden a motorcycle with a sidecar before. As he approached the first bend he could see a cyclist coming towards him and tried to pull the machine over, but it did not respond. The sidecar came up and knocked the cyclist off his bicycle. To Don's horror he realized that his victim was a policeman and not just a policeman, a sergeant to boot! The officer picked himself up and, to Don's relief, seemed all in one piece, but the bicycle looked to be in a sorry state.

"Thank goodness you're not hurt, please don't report me," begged Don.

"But when I get back to the station, they'll want to know what happened to my bike," said the sergeant, replacing his helmet and brushing the dust from his uniform. "I'm sorry lad, but I'm afraid I must report it." So Don lost his licence for an even longer time and had to pay a fine, but always the optimist, he just looked forward to being able to ride again and dreamed of competing in the TT races.

Wilf, at this time, was working on a farm at Deddington, he still yearned for the farming life.

"It's in his blood," said Louie, but after a few months he told her he could not stand it any longer.

"He's a grumpy old devil, Mum. Nothing I do is ever right."

"Come home lad," she said, knowing that Wilf was not work shy. "I don't want you to be unhappy. We'll find you a better job than that."

When he came home he looked tired and had lost weight. Life on that farm was sheer drudgery. He had been working from daylight to dark, exploited by his employer. However, before he could find a job, the Government introduced National Service and Don and Wilf, like all the other fit young lads over eighteen years old, were conscripted into the forces for two years. Louie missed her boys, but was thankful that they would not be in the same danger as poor Edwin. She made up her mind that at the first opportunity she would go to Gibraltar to visit his grave.

* * *

Louie and Henry were tidying the garden one showery afternoon and Louie's face was smeared with mud.

"Let me wipe it for you," said Henry, producing a handkerchief from his pocket.

"Whatever must I look like?" she laughed.

"I think you look lovely," he said as he wiped the smears away.

Louie looked up and saw Mildred watching them from the lounge window. "Mildred's home," she said.

"She's back earlier than I expected. I'd better go." He hurried into the house.

A fortnight later Mildred announced that she had seen a house that she liked and they would soon be moving. "It's in Upland Park Road, just off the Banbury Road, quite a nice area," she said.

Louie was astonished at her change of heart, Henry had little to say on the matter and in no time at all, they were gone.

At last the day had come for Jack to be demobbed and he was supplied with a complete outfit including a not very well cut but serviceable suit. Doreen was making cakes at the kitchen table when the door opened and a trilby hat came flying through the air and landed on the patty pans. She looked up to see Jack, who she hardly recognized in his ill-fitting pinstripe demote suit, standing in the doorway.

"Free at last!" he exclaimed as they hugged with flour from Doreen's hands showering onto the new suit. Moments later the smell of burning and smoke coming from the oven brought them back to reality and when

Jack went to change his clothes, an element of sadness crept into Doreen's happiness as she thought of her brothers having to go into the army and so many families with their loved ones still fighting the Japanese. She hardly liked to tell her friend Joan her good news as her husband, Percy, was still in a Japanese prison camp. Joan was a hairdresser and worked so very hard to bring up their little boy, Robin. It didn't seem right to be so happy. She hesitated to tell her her good news but she need not have worried, she was delighted. She reasoned that with the defeat of Germany, it would not be long before the Japanese surrendered.

Her sister, Mary, who was visiting Joan and helping to take down her blackout curtains, said she felt sure that would be the case. Mary Skinner was married and had a little girl called Ann. She also took in paying guests in her large comfortable home near the Iffley Road and like Joan, was to become a lifelong friend of Jack and Doreen.

At least Jack had a business to come back to and Alfie was pleased to be relieved of some of the work and responsibility. They were a good team, Jack was an experienced mechanic and Alfie had been trained in bodywork repair. The real difficulty was finding cars to buy in, as second-hand cars were extremely scarce. Jack sometimes found it more convenient to advertise a car from Norham Road and on one occasion there was a queue for a very old Austin Seven stretching for almost fifty yards down the road. Jack came home for lunch and walked towards the front door when a rather burly man at the head of the queue stepped out and barred his way.

"You must go to the end of the queue, Mister," he said, "I'm first for the Austin Seven."

"Well you'll have a long wait then," said Jack, taking the door key from his pocket, "because I don't intend queuing for my own car." The man moved aside apologetically and as Jack held the door open and invited him to step inside, he eagerly took a wad of notes from his pocket and nearly fell over in his haste.

"Would you like a ride in it before you make up your mind?"

"No. Just the log book." He snatched it from Jack's hand and was down the steps and into the little car in a flash. Jack watched him go and would never forget the triumphant look on his face as he drove past the queue of disappointed would-be buyers.

Alfie was a softly spoken man and never said two words if one would suffice and would take his time about that, so Jack would often send him out to buy the cars knowing that he had the patience of Job. He would stand, for what seemed like hours, silently gazing at the car till the vendor, in exasperation, invariably dropped the price. If it was a small car he had difficulty in fitting himself behind the steering wheel and when he returned to the garage Jack had to come to his aid. While he pulled and tugged and giggled, Alfie would swear to go on a diet, but he never did.

On one occasion a cocky young lad rode into the garage on his motorcycle, very full of himself. Alfie was washing a car on the forecourt and could see that Jack was getting fed up with his chatter. As the lad returned to his motorcycle, Alfie spotted his opportunity, took the soaking wet sponge from the bucket and slipped it on to the saddle as the lad stood up to kick-start the machine. He sat down heavily, the engine revving, accompanied with screams and curses. He grabbed the offending sponge but there was no one to throw it at. Alfie could move very quickly if the occasion arose. Jack had also disappeared.

Jack's younger brother, Jessy, liked to spend time at the garage and do odd jobs, keen to learn and always asking questions. One morning, Jack, having had a drink or two the night before, lost his patience, went into the office and wrote a note sealing it in an envelope. He sent Jessy shopping, telling him to hand the note to the chap behind the counter in the ironmongers on the Cowley Road.

"You'd better sit down." The salesman pointed to a stool in the corner. "It might take me a while to find this." Other clients came and went and Jessy waited and waited. After what seemed to be an eternity he was handed another envelope and told to handle it with great care and return it to Mr West. He told Jack that he could not understand why he was kept waiting so long, little did he know that Jack's note read: "PLEASE GIVE THIS LAD A LONG WAIT," and the salesman's reply: "ABOUT HALF AN HOUR!"

CHAPTER
FIVE

Jack was well known in Oxford for his mechanical skills. His father used to run a taxi and car repair business in Magdalen Road, this necessitated breaking scrap cars for parts. From an early age, Jack and his brother, Bill, were set to work in the yard. Even when he was only ten years old, one of the mechanics from a local garage sent for him as they were having difficulty tuning an engine and, as expected, he soon had the problem solved.

Now that he had his own business he was popular with the other garage proprietors, they all had difficulty in finding new stock as there was a long waiting list in England. He heard through the grapevine that there was a new Armstrong Siddeley car for sale at a reasonable price but the drawback was that it was in Jersey. Jack decided that if he spent his army gratuity he could just afford to buy it, remembering that it would be quite costly to convey it home.

"Let's go to Jersey to see this car," urged Jack. "We could spend a weekend." Doreen needed little persuading. Sylvia was thrilled, especially when Jack said they could go by train as far as Weymouth.

"Can I take Teddy?" she asked as her mother was packing the suitcases.

"Of course," said Doreen knowing she would not want to be parted from her constant companion.

Alfie drove them to the station and stood waving on the platform until they could no longer see him as he faded into the clouds of smoke and steam. Sylvia had never travelled by train before and loved every minute of the journey. She was relieved that the train ride did not bring on her usual travel sickness and watched intently through the window eager not to miss any of the unfamiliar countryside.

It was dark by the time they arrived at Weymouth and boarded the ferry. As it was a late booking they were not able to get a cabin together, so Doreen and Sylvia were to sleep at one end of the boat and Jack the other. By this time they were hungry enough to do justice to a delicious meal and were about to leave the dining room when some crockery crashed to the floor and a waiter advised them to go to their cabins. They were so enjoying themselves that they had not noticed that the other passengers had left the room with their meals only half eaten. As Doreen stood up it was a strange sensation and she knew now why her sailor brother, Edwin, walked with a rolling gait. Jack helped them both to their cabin, kissed them goodnight and, holding on to a rail for support, disappeared into the darkness. Doreen and Sylvia soon felt very ill. It was well after midnight when they fell asleep. When they woke in the morning to the sound of the ferry docking, the wind had dropped.

"Let's go and find Daddy." Sylvia was struggling into her clothes. They found Jack's cabin and Doreen knocked on the door. It was opened by a gentleman in his dressing gown who told them that he had not seen Jack and that his bunk had not been slept in.

"Perhaps Daddy's in the lounge," said Doreen. "Let's go and see." But there was no sign of him. They went to the gentlemen's toilets and asked a passing sailor to have a look inside but he told them there was no one in there. He advised them to ask the purser for help. Doreen decided to carry on searching, it was too soon to make a fuss. "I expect Daddy will turn up in time for breakfast." But he didn't. They searched high and low for over an hour. By then, Doreen was really worried and the possibility that he had fallen overboard had crossed her mind. With her heart thumping, she made her way to the purser's office.

A voice boomed out over the loudspeaker, "Would Mr Jack West please contact the purser."

A few minutes later Jack casually strolled in, wondering what the fuss was about.

"Where have you been?" Doreen's first reaction was anger. "We've been looking everywhere for you." Then she burst into tears, "I thought you were dead!"

"I just popped ashore for a little while. I've managed to exchange our ferry tickets so that we travel home on the plane. I was so sick that I spent the night in the toilets and I'm not doing that again! I've telephoned Alfie and he's going to meet us at Eastleigh Airport on Monday morning."

When they disembarked it was so warm and sunny it was like stepping into another world after the bitter cold weather they had left behind. They had booked a room in The Ommaroo Hotel and to their surprise, a liveried chauffeur with a limousine was waiting to drive them there.

They couldn't wait to see the Armstrong Siddeley and headed for the garage in St Helier. It was a lovely car and Jack soon clinched the deal.

They spent the weekend exploring the island and playing sandcastles on the beach with Sylvia. After the long years of war and the particularly hard winter it was heavenly and they wished they could have stayed longer, but Jack was anxious to get back and arrange for the car to be shipped home. So, bright and early on Monday morning, they boarded, what seemed to them a very small plane. In fact, it carried nine passengers, the pilot and co-pilot. They had not gone far when the little plane hit some air pockets and dropped like a stone. It recovered height only to repeat the process all over again, this went on at intervals throughout the flight. As Doreen clung to her seat she thought the boat ride would have been preferable but was not going to let Jack and Sylvia know how frightened she was. As they came in to land they could see Jack's Jaguar parked near the airport buildings, Alfie at the wheel. As they clambered into the car, he told them he had not expected them on such a small plane, then he saw Sylvia's Teddy at the window and knew they must be on board.

The next day Jack telephoned the shipping office to make arrangements to ship his new car home, but to his dismay he was told he would have to pay import duty which amounted to hundreds of pounds, hundreds of pounds that he had not got! When he told Doreen, who had been looking forward to a trip to Southampton to collect the car, she was devastated. Neither of them slept that night. They got up in the early hours to make tea and sat talking till dawn but could not think of a solution. When Jack came home from the garage at lunch time he told Doreen he had a plan. It so happened, he had a very old Armstrong Siddeley car in his yard.

"If we take the old car over to Jersey and switch the number plates on to the new one, we can leave the old car over there and bring the new one back."

Doreen was worried. "It's too risky, you might get into trouble."

"It's worth a try," he answered. "I'm determined to get that car home somehow."

"Let's not rush into it," pleaded Doreen. "If you telephone the garage and explain, they won't mind keeping it for a few more days."

But Jack would not hear of it. "If you don't want to come I'll get someone else."

"I'll come, but it's against my better judgement. I won't bring Sylvia this time, I'll leave her with Mother."

The snow was still lying in places by the roadside as they set off in the old Armstrong Siddeley which Alfie had cleaned and polished. The weather was improving and as they neared Southampton the cold wind had dropped and it promised to be a calm crossing. The old car was loaded onto the ferry and stood proud amongst the more modern ones and Doreen thought it was a shame to abandon the dear old thing. To their intense relief, it was a calm crossing this time. They stepped on to the quay and watched as the cars were unloaded. The chauffeur from The Ommaroo Hotel approached them smiling broadly.

"I have my own car this time," said Jack looking in the direction of the antiquated Armstrong Siddeley.

The chauffeur followed his gaze, raised his eyebrows and said, with a hint of sarcasm, "So you have, Sir."

Doreen giggled. "Sour grapes, he probably doesn't own a car of his own."

"I don't suppose he'd need one," said Jack pointing to the limousine, "if he can drive around in that all day."

Trying to keep a low profile, they left the old car round the corner from the hotel and were glad that darkness was falling as they strolled in with their overnight bags. The Ommaroo was a luxury hotel and to sink into the enormous double bed after a hot bath was pure heaven and despite their anxiety they were soon asleep.

Doreen was awake at five o'clock the next morning, she had become used to rising early in her land army days during the war. Jack usually hated getting up in the morning, but on this occasion he was soon out of bed and suggested they go for a drive around the island before breakfast to find a suitable spot to leave the old car. After they had reconnoitred practically the length and breadth of Jersey they found what they thought would be an inconspicuous spot near a creek on the far side of the island. Then, it was a speedy breakfast and off to collect the new car, taking care to leave the old one out of sight of the garage. The garage proprietor was very pleasant and wished them good luck as Jack climbed into the driving seat.

"You'd better drive this one, Doreen," he said, as he parked the shiny new car round the corner. "Then you can follow me."

Doreen was worried, she had never driven a car with an automatic gearbox before, but she was not going to tell Jack. She sat in the beautiful car with an air of confidence, but in reality her stomach churned as she remembered the narrow winding roads they had encountered earlier. He promised he would not go too fast and would keep her in his sight, so she set off in his wake. They left St Helier and headed out into the countryside, where to Doreen's horror, she watched as Jack had to reverse to negotiate a hairpin bend on a steep hill. There was no way that Doreen's car could get round in one sweep. Before she knew what was happening, she found herself running back towards a steep bank and heard an awful scraping noise. With the wheels spinning, she urged the car forward and round the bend and sped off to catch up with him, not daring to stop to see what damage she had done. When they finally reached the chosen spot Doreen hurried to the rear of the car to discover a deep dent and scratched paintwork.

"Don't worry, Alfie will soon put that right," Jack replied when Doreen plucked up the courage to tell him what had happened. He took a screwdriver out of his pocket and quickly removed the number plates from both cars putting the old plates onto the new one. Doreen was glad to relinquish the driving and soon jumped into the passenger seat.

As they drove off she glanced back sadly at the old car. "That was once someone's pride and joy. It doesn't seem right to just leave it there."

"Stop being so sentimental," Jack put his arm round her to give her a hug. He looked at his watch. "With luck, we should catch the ferry with time to spare."

With luck! thought Doreen. *We're going to need a lot of that in the next few hours.*

There were admiring glances as the shiny new car was loaded onto the ferry and Doreen and Jack went aboard. It was a beautiful day for the time of year and they stood on deck holding hands and watched Jersey fading from view as they headed for the open sea. They were so nervous that the voyage seemed interminable, but at last they had docked in Southampton and were taken to a large building where the Armstrong Siddeley was parked. Three men in uniform were peering under the bonnet and then in the boot. Jack swore under his breath, he knew the game was up! After conferring, one of the men came over to them and said they would be keeping the car for further investigation as there was a problem concerning the engine number. He advised them to go home on the train and wait for the result of their enquiries.

When they arrived home, Doreen went straight to Bradmore Road where she found Louie and Sylvia in the kitchen baking cakes. Louie had been told that the trip to Jersey was simply to collect a car, now it was time for Doreen to tell her the whole story.

"Why didn't you tell me?" she said. "I could have helped you to raise the money."

A few weeks later they received a summons ordering both Doreen and Jack to attend the court in Southampton in a month's time. Jack was charged with attempting to evade import duty on a car. Doreen was horrified to read in the small print that a verdict of guilty could result in up to two years in prison. She told Louie that afternoon, knowing she would want to be kept informed, she had promised her "no more secrets".

Jack went to his solicitor, Bunny Cole, who was highly acclaimed in the Oxford area. He stressed the seriousness of what Jack had done and said they would need to employ a first-class barrister to defend him.

"I know the very man," he said. "If anyone can get you off, he can, though he will have his work cut out."

Later that afternoon, he telephoned Jack to confirm that he had engaged Mr Marcus Quinten KC to defend him and wished him luck. "I'm afraid it will be goodbye to the car, they're bound to confiscate that, even if you're found not guilty."

It was the day of the court case, which was to be heard in the afternoon. Bunny Cole travelled to Southampton with Doreen and Jack so that they could discuss the case on the way. They arrived early at the court, so while Jack was talking to his barrister, Doreen wandered off and found her way into the public gallery. The case in progress concerned a seaman who had been found guilty of stealing two tins of fruit. Doreen was shocked when he was sentenced to six months in prison, it seemed a harsh sentence for such a petty crime. She prayed that Jack's case was not heard by such an unsympathetic judge.

Doreen returned to the reception area where Jack introduced her to Marcus Quinten who greeted her with a firm handshake. He was a handsome man, very tall, and behind his enormous horn-rimmed spectacles his kind twinkling eyes radiated a reassuring smile.

The court usher announced that it was time to make their way to the court room. Doreen gave Jack's hand a squeeze and whispered, "Good luck." When they were shown to their respective places she noticed that Marcus Quinten had donned his wig and towered head and shoulders above the prosecuting barrister. *He certainly looks impressive*, she thought, *but "handsome is as handsome does"*.

"All rise!" Everyone stood up while the judge took his seat. Doreen gasped, it was the same stern judge from the previous case.

The prosecuting counsel stated that it had been Jack's intention, from the start, to cheat and deceive Customs and Excise so that he would not have to pay import duty. He opened proceedings by calling two of the customs officers to give evidence. The car was obviously almost new, with only a few miles on the clock, whereas the registration number belonged to an older vehicle, also the engine and chassis numbers differed from the ones on the documents. The garage owner also testified that he had sold the car to Jack West but it then had a different registration number. As the evidence built up it seemed that Jack was no more than a devious villain and Doreen longed to stand up and tell everyone how wrong this was, but when Marcus Quinten put his case for the defence and Doreen was called to give evidence, her mouth went dry and she started to tremble. However, she managed to pull herself together and speak out clearly when answering the questions from both barristers. She emphasized Jack's plea that when he spent all his savings on the car, they had no idea that he would also have to pay import duty as they thought Jersey was part of the United Kingdom. The judge nodded and looked thoughtful. Throughout the case Jack had been sitting quietly, smartly dressed in his Harris tweed jacket and grey flannel trousers, and when giving his evidence he remained composed and explained his predicament with great sincerity.

Marcus Quinten summed up with a brilliant speech and finally pointed to Jack and said, "Does this man look like a smuggler to you?"

They had an agonizing wait of an hour before they were called back into court to hear the verdict of not guilty. They could hardly believe their ears and Doreen was soon in Jack's arms with tears of relief streaming down her face. Bunny and Marcus came over to shake hands, obviously delighted with the result.

"It's just a shame you'll lose that lovely car," said Bunny. No sooner had he spoken than a court official came towards them.

"Mr West? If you would like to make your way to Southampton Police Station they'll tell you where you can collect your car." Jack thanked him casually, but when the man was out of earshot, he let out a whoop of joy and his face lit up in a broad grin. Bunny and Marcus Quinten looked at each other, their expressions of disbelief turning to smiles.

"Tell me I'm not dreaming!" Doreen gasped.

Marcus Quinten was anxious to be on his way as he had a long drive back to London. Doreen telephoned

Louie to tell her the good news. They collected the car, then took Bunny to a local hotel for an excellent meal before heading for home, the two men in the Armstrong Siddeley and Doreen following in the Jaguar. It was late in the evening and pouring with rain. The glass of sherry she had enjoyed to celebrate their good fortune made her feel drowsy and she often lost sight of the tail lights on Jack's car. Not being too sure of the way she was thankful when, at last, they reached Oxford. She drove straight to Bradmore Road to collect Sylvia, Louie and Janet eagerly waiting to hear about the court case.

CHAPTER
SIX

Sylvia was five years old and it was time for her to start school. Doreen hated the thought of it, it was another milestone in her life. She talked it over with Jack and they decided that a private school would be best. They chose Greycotes School which was on the Banbury Road, not too far away. When they met the charming headmistress they felt that Sylvia would be happy there. However, when Doreen walked with her to the door on her first day, dressed in her smart new uniform, she turned and fled and was half way home before her mother could catch up with her. After much persuading she relented and went back. Doreen made sure not to let go of her hand until a teacher came to take her into class. Then she walked home, occasionally glancing over her shoulder, half expecting that Sylvia might be following her. She never enjoyed the routine of school life and, like her mother, longed for the last lesson of the day to be over so that she could run home.

It was a bitter cold winter morning in 1946, it had been snowing on and off for a week and some roads were impassable. Doreen had started to tackle her morning chores, riddling the big boiler and shovelling on more coke, when the doorbell rang. She hurried to answer it and was startled to find a policeman standing on her doorstep.

"Are you Mrs Doreen West?" he asked.

"Yes, I am," she said, she could feel her heart racing. "What's the matter? Has Jack had an accident?"

"Could I come in for a moment, Madam?"

She took him into the lounge and waited expectantly. By the look on his face and the way he hesitated before speaking she knew his errand was not a pleasant one.

"Is your father's name Algernon Hutt?"

"Yes," Doreen answered. "Has something happened to him?"

"I'm afraid he was found dead last night in a field on his farm. The doctor thinks he probably had a heart attack. I'm sorry to bring you such sad news."

Though she had not seen her father for some time, Doreen's legs went quite weak. "Have you told my mother?" she asked.

"No. I came to you first," he said.

"I think it would be best if I tell her," Doreen suggested, to the constable's relief.

He said he must be on his way and as she opened the door the bitter wind blew a flurry of snow into the hall. She watched anxiously as he nearly lost his footing down the steps, his car skidded on the snowy surface before driving away.

Doreen went straight to her mother's house. Louie looked surprised but pleased to see her. "Whatever's brought you out so early in this weather?" she asked. "Let's go into the kitchen, it's warmer there."

"Can we have a cup of tea?" Doreen wanted to make sure that Louie was sitting down before telling her the shocking news. She had no sooner told her, when the telephone rang. It was the family solicitor, Cecil Rose from Faringdon, asking if Louie could call on him that evening.

Jack said he had better drive them, in view of the weather, but Doreen thought they would be all right as it had stopped snowing. She drove off in the late afternoon to collect Louie and Janet and headed for Faringdon, armed with a shovel in case they got stuck in the snow. It was not a pleasant journey and they all breathed a sigh of relief when they pulled up in Mr Rose's drive, to be met at the door by his wife. Mrs Rose was a kindly soul, she hugged them and ushered them into the drawing room where they were soon joined by her husband who, after expressing his condolences, proceeded to push the settee and chairs nearer to the blazing fire.

"You must be frozen. What a night!" he said as a maid entered with a tray of drinks. "I don't know how much you know about Algy's death, but I understand it was a heart attack."

"That's what the policeman told us," said Louie, "but that's all we know."

"Well, I understand he went out with his gun at midday, taking his two dogs. When he had not returned after dark, his housekeeper raised the alarm and some neighbouring farmers went to find him. It was snowing heavily and, with only lanterns to light their way, it took them a long time to find his body. His two dogs were guarding him and refused to let anyone near. The neighbours were wonderful and when they had pacified the faithful dogs, they laid him on a gate and carried him back to the farmhouse. It was a great shock to his housekeeper, Beth."

"I'll go to the farm tomorrow," said Louie, "to see what I can do to help."

"It's your farm now, Louie," said Mr Rose. "I'm going to tell you something I've never mentioned before. About two years ago, Algy came to my office and told me he wanted to alter his will. It was market day and I think he had had a few drinks. He told me he was going to leave everything to a dog's home. I told him that if he did not leave his family what was rightfully theirs he would have to find another solicitor because I would not act for him. He stormed out of my office and I am certain the will has never been changed."

Louie was overcome. "How can I ever express my gratitude Mr Rose? We'll be forever in your debt."

It had started to snow again, so they thought they had better get home as soon as possible. The roads had become treacherous and Doreen had difficulty in steering the car. In the darkness visibility was practically nil. The windscreen wipers could not cope with the heavy snow so they had to stop frequently to clear it by hand. It was late into the night when they finally reached their destination safe and sound.

Due to the bad weather, The Catherine Wheel had few visitors, so Janet and Babs were allowed time off. Janet said she could run the guest house while Louie was away and Babs offered to go with her to help at the farm, but first they had to get there! Doreen drove them. Sylvia

65

and her granny shared a blanket on the back seat and Janet went too in case Doreen needed help on her drive home. The journey seemed to take forever and by the time they reached the farm gates, snow had drifted across the long drive that led across the fields to the farm, but the car managed to slip and slide its way through. When they finally arrived the front door opened and the two labradors, Cloud and Sky, bounded out to meet them followed by Beth, who hustled everyone indoors. A blazing log fire was a sight for sore eyes and drew them to it like a magnet. Sylvia was in her element curled up on the hearthrug with the two dogs, but it was soon time to leave as Doreen and Janet were anxious to get on their way before darkness fell.

"Do you want to see your father?" Louie asked them but they shook their heads.

"I'd rather remember him as he was when he was alive," said Doreen. Janet nodded in agreement.

"I hope the boys will be here in time for the funeral, I heard on the wireless that a lot of trains have had to be cancelled."

Unbeknown to them, Don had been posted abroad and did not learn of his father's death till after the funeral. Wilf was stationed at Catterick Camp. His journey took eighteen hours and he arrived only just in time to see his father laid to rest in the little churchyard at Buckland. Due to the bad weather few people were able to attend the funeral or even send flowers, so it was a sad end for Algy, though his family treasured memories of him from happier times.

After the funeral the weather closed in and the driveway to the farm was completely blocked. Wilf was unable to return to camp and the two farm workers could not get to work. Wilf and Babs looked after the store cattle in the barn and took it in turns to try to milk the house-cow, which proved difficult as she did not trust strangers and was loath to let them near her. Poultry had always been Louie's responsibility in her farming days, so she took over the chickens and ducks. Food was starting to run low with four of them to feed. Louie thought they may soon have to kill one of the hens, but was reluctant to do so while they were still laying.

One morning, Wilf asked Babs if she had ever fired a gun.

"No, never," she replied.

"Come on then, I'll teach you," he said, taking Algy's 12 bore from the rack in the kitchen and handing a smaller gun to Babs, who took it with some trepidation.

"Now be careful Wilf," said Louie, "and don't be long or I shall worry, the snow is very deep in places where it's drifted."

"We'll be all right," he said, fastening his army greatcoat. "What's the betting we'll have rabbit stew for dinner tomorrow?"

A blast of cold air hit them as they opened the back door. Louie watched them from the window as they headed towards the meadow at the rear of the house and in the distance she could see Wilf holding the gun in a firing position, then the sound of a gunshot.

"That's our rabbit stew," she said to Beth, who was sitting as close to the fire as she could, with her feet resting on the brass fender. Louie knew that Wilf was a fine marksman.

Takes after his dad in that way, she thought and knew that Algy would have been proud of his youngest son. *He taught him well, I wish things had been different.* The two women sat chatting and drinking tea.

"How did you get on with Algy?" Louie asked, "I hope he didn't lose his temper with you."

"He was the perfect gentleman, but I knew when things didn't go his way, he would shout at the men but he knew better than to upset me," Beth gave a wry smile, "and in case you're wondering, there was no hanky-panky. He was still very much in love with you and would, I know, have given the world to have you and the children back." She lifted another log from the basket and piled it onto the fire.

"I couldn't risk it again," Louie told her. "I left him when the boys were young and we went back to him when he promised he would change. Don and Wilf were strong little lads by then and they worked hard all summer on the farm, as I did. When the haymaking and harvesting was finished, however, he threw us out again with not so much as a thank you."

"I didn't know," Beth replied. "He wouldn't have told me things like that, when he spoke of you it was to praise you. He told me how proud he was that his wife was such a wonderful mother and hostess."

"You must have thought I was a dreadful wife to leave him on his own," said Louie.

"Not really, but I must admit I sometimes felt a bit jealous. I've been a widow for many years, my husband was killed in the first world war and since then I've worked as a housekeeper, keeping other people's homes spick-and-span, always longing for a place of my own. Now I'm sixty five I shall go and live with my sister, who's rather frail."

"I think Algy was very lucky to have found you and I'll always be grateful for what you've done. Is there anything in the house you'd like to keep in his memory?"

Beth looked around the room, "I've always loved this picture." She had chosen a water-colour of a country scene that Louie remembered buying in Witney to cheer up a bare wall at Mill Farm, but she was happy for Beth to have it.

Meanwhile, Wilf had shot two rabbits and the bitter cold was creeping into their bones so they decided to head for home. As they neared the farmhouse Wilf explained to Babs how to break open the gun and take out the cartridges. By now, her hands were very cold and perhaps her senses were not as sharp as they might have been, but somehow she caught a numb finger in the trigger and the gun went off with a deafening report. Wilf looked down at his feet, and, not two inches from his toe, was a hole in the snow where the shot had landed.

"My God, Babs!" he looked at her in astonishment, but her face was white with shock so he put his arm round her and laughed. "You nearly got me my ticket out of the army, I've heard of 'shooting yourself in the foot', you nearly did it for me." He took the gun from her shaking hands. "Come on, I bet tea's ready and I think we could do with a cup."

As they trudged back through the snow Wilf realized what a lucky escape he had had, if Babs had been holding the gun at a different angle it could have been curtains for him. "I don't think we should tell Mother," he said. "No need to worry her." He spotted Louie at the window and triumphantly held the rabbits aloft for her to see.

Still no sign of a let up in the weather and no sign of Don, they knew he would not be able to get to the farm but wondered why he had not telephoned. At last, after about ten days they heard from him. He had been stationed in Trieste and had managed to get compassionate leave. He was telephoning from Oxford and would be with them as soon as possible.

At the farm, everyone spent their spare time clearing the long drive to make it passable. No more snow had fallen and snowploughs had cleared the main road, so Louie was hoping they would be able to get to Faringdon the next day. Wilf managed to start the engine of Algy's Wolseley, which had not been used for some time, but Louie had not driven for a while and was apprehensive about driving such a powerful car. She was relieved, however, when Babs offered to take the wheel. The main roads were surprisingly clear and she soon whirled them into Faringdon and parked outside Chamberlain's Grocery store, where they bought enough provisions to replenish the larder and returned to the farm just in time for Don's arrival.

As the weather improved the farm hands returned to work and Beth said a sad goodbye to the country life to go and live with her sister. The boys would soon have to go back to their regiments but Babs was in no hurry to leave as there were still very few visitors at The Catherine Wheel and, like Janet, she did not have to return to Henley for a few weeks. Louie took the oportunity to move to the farm for a while. She had already grown quite fond of the place, as Algy had predicted, but she knew she could not live there alone and the children had to have a share in the proceeds according to his will so it would have to be put up for auction. To wake up to the country sounds: the cockerel crowing, a pheasant calling in the distance and the cattle bellowing for their breakfast, brought back memories of happy times with Algy and she had to admit he had chosen well with Home Farm. She wished, in spite of everything, that he could have lived longer to spend more time in these lovely surroundings.

Wilf's compassionate leave had come to an end and he had to return to camp and Don left the following day to travel back to Trieste. With only fifteen months apart in their ages they were very close friends as well as brothers and Louie knew the parting would be hard for them. After losing Edwin she dreaded goodbyes to her sons in uniform, but at least the war had ended. She made up her mind to go to Gibraltar to visit Edwin's grave, but thought she would probably have to wait till after the farm sale. However, when Babs heard of her plans she suggested that Louie take her trip sooner rather than later, confident that she could manage the farm herself now that the farm hands had returned and she felt that Louie really needed a holiday. Louie talked it over with Janet and Doreen a few days later and was

71

delighted when Janet said she would like to go with her. Much as Doreen would have loved to go, there was no way she could leave Jack and Sylvia, so she decided to take on some extra temporary staff and run both guest houses.

CHAPTER
SEVEN

Louie and Janet started to make plans for their trip, their first task was to book a passage to Gibraltar. They were fortunate to get berths on the SS Franconia, which would be sailing in a fortnight.

Next, they had to shop for suitable clothes as their wardrobes were somewhat depleted with rationing through the war years. They decided to visit Webbers, a large department store in the High Street in Oxford. Louie had gone through to the dress department while Janet, who was looking at some swimwear, put her belongings on the counter for a moment while she took a bathing costume from a hanger. Still gazing at the attractive garment, she put her hand down to pick up her new handbag, which she had bought especially for the trip and contained a considerable amount of money and her cheque book, to discover that it had disappeared as clean as a whistle! There were not many people in the store and she could not recall seeing anyone near to her. Louie blamed herself for not staying with her but this was obviously the work of a cunning opportunist. They telephoned Janet's bank manager from the store to let him know what had happened. However, two days later a young woman went into the bank and asked to cash one of her cheques. The cashier asked her to wait while she went to query it.

The woman seemed annoyed, turned to the other people in the queue and said, "I don't think I'll wait." She calmly walked out of the bank and by the time the cashier returned she had disappeared down the Banbury Road, never to be seen again. At last, all was ready and at Louie's suggestion, Doreen drove them down to Southampton in Algy's Wolseley and was to use it while she was away. She stood on the dock with Sylvia and waved goodbye to Louie and Janet as the Franconia left port to head for Gibraltar. On the way home she took the opportunity to stop the car in the New Forest so that Sylvia could watch the wild ponies.

When they arrived in Gibraltar after a most enjoyable voyage, Louie and Janet hailed a taxi and asked the driver, who seemed to understand English, to take them to a good hotel. He drove them to a run-down area and deposited them outside a seedy looking building with a large sign: THE GRAND HOTEL. They looked at each other and without a word picked up their belongings and started to walk. They had trudged quite a way before finding a policeman, he recommended The Rock Hotel and told them it was only round the corner and helped to carry their luggage the rest of the way.

"This is more like it!" said Louie as they reached the main entrance and a liveried doorman took charge of their suitcases. The policeman had advised them well, it was a superb hotel with every luxury and the food was excellent.

As soon as they were settled, they arranged a trip to the cemetery. They found their way to Edwin's grave. There was a stone cross with his name and that of another sailor buried with him, which was a shock, but apparently there was not enough room on the rock for all the servicemen to have individual graves. They sat for a long time in that peaceful garden. At last, Louie had seen the final resting place of her beloved eldest son.

The weather was wonderful and despite the sad reason for their visit they were thoroughly enjoying their holiday. During their stay at the hotel they met many interesting people. One of the guests was Captain John Sizes, who was the captain of an oil tanker which was anchored off-shore and he would often invite them to spend the day on board where they were given star treatment. The sea was so warm that Janet was able to swim and then they would sit on the deck of the huge vessel and bask in the sunshine. John spent any spare time he had with them and seemed to look forward to their company.

One day, he took them to Tangier in his launch where they strolled around the local bazaar. Louie was amazed to see beautiful carpets and rugs for sale in abundance for reasonable prices, in England they were very expensive and not readily available. She thought they would cheer up Number Ten no end and would also make excellent gifts. One after another, the salesman spread the carpets in front of her, each one more lovely than the one before, so by the time Captain Sizes came to see how she was getting on, she had chosen seven large Indian carpets and as many rugs.

"You have to barter with these people," he said and proceeded to haggle with the salesman till her final bill was greatly reduced. The carpets were loaded onto handcarts and trundled to the launch. John Sizes looked on with amusement as Louie took charge of the operation keeping a watchful eye on her precious purchases.

Louie and Janet took some lovely trips into Spain and fell in love with the town of Malaga and its pretty dark haired children, the little girls in beautifully embroidered frocks. The flowers, especially geraniums, grew in profusion, sadly reminding Louie that since the war years many English gardens had become neglected. She said she would have liked to live there, but knew in her heart she would never leave England and her family.

The time had come for them to leave for home. They said goodbye to John Sizes and thanked him for making their holiday so special and they all vowed to keep in touch.

Doreen received a telephone call from Louie asking her to collect them from Southampton. They were returning home on RMS *Dunnattor Castle*.

"Has Jack got a trailer?" Louie asked. "I seem to have got rather a lot of extra luggage and I don't think we shall get it all in the car." Doreen laughed. *I expect she's exaggerating*, she thought.

The very night before Louie and Janet were due to arrive home Jack told Doreen that someone had stolen the spotlight from Louie's Wolseley and there was no way he could get another before her trip to Southampton.

"Well I won't need it, will I?" she replied. "It's a trailer Mum says we need, but I think she was joking."

"Well I haven't got one anyway," he said.

The next morning Doreen set out good and early, leaving Jack to take care of Sylvia.

Doreen enjoyed using the Wolseley, any car was a pleasure to drive after the heavy electric milk float she had had to cope with when in the land army. She reached Southampton in good time and turned into the gates of the dock from where she was hoping to watch the *Dunnattor Castle* sail into port, but the ship was already alongside. There, sitting on a pile of large packages, were her mother and sister. *She wasn't joking after all.* After hugs and kisses Louie wanted to know where the trailer was and where had her spotlight gone?

"Jack doesn't own a trailer and unfortunately your spotlight has been stolen. Jack has ordered a new one and will put it on as soon as he can," Doreen explained, quite surprised that her mother had noticed that it was missing.

"Mother's been awake all night worrying about getting the carpets home," Janet confided to Doreen when they were alone.

With a great deal of pushing, shoving and grunting they loaded as many packages as they could into the car. A friendly docker told them where they could store the remainder safely till Doreen and Louie's return the next day to collect the rest. The carpets proved to be of excellent quality and adorned the family homes for years to come.

It was a Sunday afternoon and it was Bernard's birthday. Jane and Louie were in the kitchen preparing a special tea and the rest of the house was empty. All the guests were out, but they had promised to be back by five o'clock for the birthday celebration. Jane was looking forward to giving Bernard his present, she had bought him a smart cravat. Ronald Colman had been wearing one in the last film they had seen together and she thought it made him look very distinguished.

The front doorbell rang. "Shall I go?" Jane offered as Louie's hands were covered in flour. She opened the door to find a young woman and a little boy about four years old.

"I hope I've come to the right house. Does Bernard Jones live here?" she said.

"Yes, but I'm afraid he's out," said Jane. "Can I help you?"

"Oh dear!" the woman seemed anxious. "We've travelled down from Yorkshire specially to see him on his birthday. I'm Aileen Jones, Bernard's wife, and this is his son, Stephen." She fondly stroked the little boy's dark curly hair.

Jane was stunned.

It took her a moment to recover from the shock. "Please come in," she said. "I think he'll be back soon. You can wait in the lounge and I'll tell Mrs Hutt that you're here." She showed them into the lounge and ran to find Louie. As she was telling her what had happened, she burst into tears and fled up the stairs to her room.

Louie took Aileen and Stephen a pot of tea and soon made them feel at home. "I'm sure Bernard will be thrilled to see you," she said. "We were just making him a special tea, I hope you'll join us. Will you be staying for a while? I can soon arrange accommodation."

"We must go home tomorrow," said Aileen, "but it would be nice to stay here tonight, if it's not too much trouble? I've got some good news for Bernard, I'm hoping he can move back home soon. You know, of course, that he had to come to Oxford to find work, there were no jobs available in Malton. Now that the war is over, my father is expanding his business and there's a job waiting for him. I can't tell you how much we've missed him."

By tea time, Bernard had been reunited with his family, Jane had regained her composure and a happy time was had by all.

It took Bernard a month to work out his notice with the bank and then it was time for him to leave. He gave Louie and Jane a bunch of flowers each. "For my two best girl friends," he laughed and kissed them both, before loading his luggage into a taxi and waving goodbye. Up to the time he left, Jane had seemed cheerful, but after he had gone she became very subdued.

About three weeks later, Olive happened to be looking out of her window, which overlooked the road, when she saw a car pull-up outside Number Ten. A young couple got out and helped Jane, who was wrapped in a travelling rug, out of the back seat. Something seemed odd, and then Olive realized that they were all soaking wet.

She hurried down to the hall and called out, "Louie, I think you'd better come to the door."

They helped Jane inside, she was not only drenched, but reeked of stagnant water. "I'll take her straight upstairs for a hot bath," said Olive.

The young lady told Louie that they had been walking along the tow path beside the canal when they saw Jane jump from the bridge and disappear under the water. Her husband had jumped in and dragged her to the bank, and together, they pulled her out. They did not want to involve the police as she seemed so distressed, so thought it best to bring her straight home. Louie thanked them and took note of their address, she was sure Jane would want to thank them at a later date. They hurried home to change out of their wet clothes.

Jane was still shivering and crying after a hot bath and plenty of sweet tea, so Louie gave her a glass of brandy and they tucked her into bed with a hot water bottle. "I've done such a silly thing," she sobbed, "and I've given you all so much trouble."

"Don't upset yourself," said Olive. "Anyone can have an accident."

"But it wasn't an accident," Jane cried. "Since Bernard left, I've been so depressed, I felt I had nothing to live for."

"You must get a good night's sleep," said Louie. "Then, when you're rested and feeling better, you'll have to pull yourself together and get on with life. There'll be plenty to look forward to and Olive and I won't tell anyone what happened."

The atomic bomb had been dropped on Hiroshima and at last the war with Japan had ended. Doreen's friend, Joan, was over the moon, her husband, Percy, was on his way home at last after being incarcerated in a Japanese prison camp for what must have seemed an eternity, it was in fact three and a half years.

80

After weeks of waiting, Joan had a telephone call from Percy to say that he had arrived in England and was in a demote centre in Amersham. His friend, Dickie Bird, who was also a prisoner of war, was with him. They were to be issued with railway passes and then they could return home in a few days.

Dickie Bird's wife, Peggy, and father ran a newsagent shop in North Oxford. Joan contacted them to tell them the good news.

"I'm going to phone the demote centre," said Mr Bird. "They might let them come home straight away if I collect them in my car."

Permission for a speedy demobilization was granted and Joan, Robin and Peggy travelled with Mr Bird to Amersham. When they arrived at the centre a soldier directed them to the Naafi where they would find Percy and Dickie. It was a tearful, emotional meeting. The two young men were in such a poor state of health that their families barely recognized them. After years of starvation they appeared to be no more than walking skeletons and the long journey home had exhausted them.

After leaving the prison camp, they had travelled by ship to the west coast of America. On this stage of the journey some of the men had become so mentally unbalanced by their unaccustomed freedom that they committed suicide by jumping overboard. Their families must have been devastated to lose them after expecting them to be brought safely home. They then endured a long journey by train to the east coast where they boarded *The Queen Mary*, which had been commandeered as a troop ship, to sail to England.

At least they were alive and so thankful to be home. When it was time for them to leave Percy and Dickie took up so little room in the car that, even with their kit, the six passengers fitted in easily. As they drove along Percy searched in his pockets and found a small package which he gave to Robin. It was a penknife inscribed: QUEEN MARY. The young lad was to treasure it all his life.

After Percy had been home for a while and was feeling stronger he made frequent visits to his old pals in Norham Road. On one occasion Jack told him about the theft of the spotlight from Louie's car. It had become her main topic of conversation, almost to the point of obsession. When Louie finally met him, they shook hands rather formally then he gave her a hug.

"How are you, Spotlight Lou?" he asked with a twinkle in his eye. You could never be offended by Percy's cheeky humour and Louie thought it was hilarious and as far as Percy was concerned, "Spotlight Lou" she remained.

Joan was happy to have her family complete again, but sadly, her sister Mary's marriage had ended in divorce. During the day while Mary was at work, her daughter Ann was looked after by her mother-in-law. She was employed in the admissions department at the Radcliffe Infirmary and part of her duties involved taking the particulars of new patients. When, one day, a nurse asked her to go to the Emergency Ward, cubicle three, to register a new admission, she had the shock of her life when she drew back the curtain to find Ann lying on the bed. She was obviously very ill and in pain and her grandmother was with her, holding her hand. The specialist diagnosed appendicitis and Ann was rushed to the operating theatre. She soon made a complete recovery, but Mary could never forget the day she left her daughter happily playing and the nightmare of finding her dangerously ill a few hours later.

Two months had passed since Jane had been pulled from the canal. She still seemed very downhearted, staying in her room in the evenings with little conversation and rarely a smile. She had not even visited her beloved cinema.

"I think it's time Jane stopped moping around. She's getting on my nerves," said Olive one evening, after Jane had returned to her room.

"I wish there was something we could do to cheer her up," said Louie.

"You leave her to me," Olive sounded resolute. "I'll sort her out." She then disappeared up the stairs to knock on Jane's door. "I'd like you to come with me tomorrow evening to meet some of my friends. Be ready by seven o'clock and dress in your prettiest clothes." Jane was so taken aback that she agreed to go, though she did not think Olive's friends would be interested in meeting her.

After the two ladies had set off the next evening, Louie started to have misgivings. She was curious to know where Olive had taken Jane and hoped that she would not feel out of place, which would only make her more depressed.

Louie need not have worried. The following morning Jane was tapping on the kitchen door, full of enthusiasm.

"You'll never guess where we went yesterday," she said. "Olive took me to The Cedars Convalescent Home to meet some of the patients. Apparently she visits them most evenings and does what she can to cheer them up. They are mostly servicemen with severe war wounds, some have lost limbs and some are blind. She reads to them, helps feed them and arranges visits from their families. I could tell that both the staff and the patients think the world of her. They let me help, reading and making hot drinks and the evening flew by. Those men are so brave, it made me ashamed that I've been so selfish lately."

"Well I never!" Louie was astonished. "I often wondered where Olive went in the evenings. Why didn't she tell us?"

"I don't know," said Jane. "She's invited me to go back with her whenever I like, so I'll go this evening. I'm sure there's plenty I can do."

Jane joined Olive on her trips to The Cedars most evenings and weekends. Until recently the two women never seemed to get on that well, being as different as chalk and cheese, but now they had a common interest their friendship blossomed.

A few months later Olive asked Louie if she thought Jack might have a reliable car to sell her. She particularly wanted a saloon. Jack left word that he did not have anything suitable at the moment. The only saloon he had would be far too big as it was a Daimler, but he would contact her as soon as he had something smaller.

"I don't know why he thinks a Daimler would be too big for me," she said. "It sounds ideal. I want my passengers to travel in comfort."

"I didn't know you could drive," said Louie.

"I can't, but that shouldn't be any problem, should it? I was hoping you'd teach me."

Louie was aghast. "But I haven't done much driving lately. I don't think I'd make a very good teacher."

"I'm sure you'd manage. Just as long as you stop me from bumping into things till I get the hang of it. It's all in a good cause. I want to take the boys from The Cedars on some outings and I could collect their relations from the station when they come to visit them."

"I'll do my best," said Louie. "Though the car may be quite expensive."

"That's not a problem," said Olive. "When my fiancé was killed at the beginning of the war he left me some money in his will. I thought this would be a good way to use some of it."

The more Louie learned of Olive the more she realized that she was an exceptional lady and the simple task of learning to drive in a Daimler limousine should not be a problem. Jack arranged the necessary paperwork for Olive and delivered the gleaming black car to Number Ten, where it stood prominently on the front drive.

Whenever they had some spare time, Olive and Louie would set off in the big car, weaving, jumping and stalling their way down the road. Quite often Jane could be seen peering out of the rear window. Gradually their exit from Bradmore Road became smoother and it was obvious that Olive was getting the hang of it. They combined the driving lessons with shopping trips or visits to friends to save petrol and Louie had to admit that she was enjoying their outings. When the grand day came that Olive passed her test she was almost disappointed.

"Now we'll teach Jane to drive," said Olive. So the three ladies set off again. This time it took a little longer!

The day after Jane passed her driving test, she celebrated with a visit to the local hairdressing salon where she had her hair cut, permed and set into the latest fashionable style. "I must look my best for 'the boys'," she said.

The large car was a great success. The strongest of the patients from The Cedars were taken on outings to local places of interest including Blenheim Palace and Whipsnade Zoo and some of the more poorly managed short trips to Bradmore Road to have tea with Louie. Regular visits to Oxford Railway Station to pick up tired friends and relations and their luggage after long train journeys and take them to their lodgings or straight to the Cedars were very much appreciated.

CHAPTER
EIGHT

The time had come for the farm to be sold. The frequent journeys between Carswell and Bradmore Road were becoming a strain on Louie and she could not expect Janet to run the guest house for much longer. She was going to miss the livestock on the farm, especially the poultry. She kept a few hens in her garden at Number Ten but it did not compare with the pleasure of watching the hens scratching around in the farmyard with the ducks and geese.

Babs was such a lovely companion, always so content. They liked to take a walk together round the farm in the evenings checking on the animals with Sky and Cloud, the labrador dogs, bounding on in front.

"I don't think they'll like living in the town," said Louie. Babs agreed, she too had become very fond of them.

The next day they set off into Faringdon to visit a local estate agent to decide on a date to put the farm stock up for auction. Michaelmas Day, at the end of September, was the obvious choice and would give them just enough time to make all the arrangements.

The big day had come and thankfully the weather was fine. The implements were lined up in the home paddock and the animals were herded into pens made of hurdles, each with a round label stuck on its rump recording their auction number. It all seemed so final. When the two horses were led out of their stables it was the last straw and Janet and Doreen, close to tears, went into the house in search of sugar knobs for them. Thankfully, a neighbour, who they knew to be a kind man, bought both of them and as the auctioneer banged his gavel down on the table they breathed a sigh of relief. They all returned to Oxford that night, with the livestock gone there was nothing to keep them at the farm.

Louie had made sure that the farm workers had found employment elsewhere before giving up the farm, which now had to be auctioned. This was to take place at the Red Lion Hotel in Faringdon and there was much speculation in the weeks leading up to the sale as to how much it would fetch and who would buy it. Louie had no idea how much the property was worth. The room was packed and when the auctioneer closed the bidding at thirteen thousand pounds she felt that a chapter of her life had closed and it was time to start afresh.

Mr Rose was sitting beside her on the rostrum. "It's a very good price," he told her, taking her arm and beckoning to the girls to follow. "Come home with me for a chat, Mrs Rose will have the tea ready."

By the time Babs and Janet were ready to return to work at the Catherine Wheel they were told that their positions had been taken so they started to look for employment elsewhere. It transpired that there were two vacancies at The Whately Hall Hotel in Banbury. Louie suggested that they apply assuring them that she could manage the guest house with her daily help.

Janet and Babs, as smart as new pins, went for their interview and were promptly accepted, Janet as receptionist and Babs as secretary.

Louie, meanwhile, advertised in the *Oxford Times* for a live-in assistant. A lady called Miss Fanny Browning applied for the post. She seemed keen to take on the work and though middle-aged, quite sprightly. She had been divorced and had reverted to her maiden name. Louie was a little apprehensive as she had rather a daunting manner but put that down to nervousness and offered her the job. Fanny did not need a second asking and arrived next day with all her worldly goods in one suitcase.

The first chore she set herself was to clean the large gas cooker, a job Louie detested, but Fanny was seemingly enjoying herself, she was certainly taking her time. Louie was getting quite worried as it was time to start cooking lunch but still the cooker was in pieces and Fanny was happily scrubbing away. Another half hour went by and she did not seem to have made much headway. Louie decided she could wait no longer, she liked to be punctual with the meals, so she took the bull by the horns, stripped up her sleeves and started to replace the top of the cooker.

"Do you mind if I give you a hand? I really must start cooking now," said Louie firmly. This little incident sparked off a tantrum and Fanny flounced out of the kitchen, slamming the door behind her. Louie hurriedly assembled the cooker. By the time she had prepared the meal there was still no sign of her. She served the guests, ate her own lunch and went shopping. When she returned Fanny was sitting in the kitchen drinking a cup of tea. *I'm not putting up with this behaviour*, thought Louie as she waited for an apology, but none came so she went to her sitting room where she could be on her own, read her newspaper and collect her thoughts. After a while there was a knock on the door and Fanny appeared with a tray of tea which she placed on a small table beside Louie who thanked her and proceeded to pour herself a cup. Fanny turned and left the room without a word. As she sipped her tea in the privacy of her own room Louie wondered whether she had taken on more than she had bargained for when offering this petulant lady employment, but the next morning she was behaving quite normally.

An overdue letter arrived from Don, it was very short and the writing looked rather shaky. He told his mother that he was recovering from an attack of meningitis and hoped he would soon be sent home to England to convalesce. The word "meningitis" struck fear into Louie's heart but the fact that he was on the road to recovery helped to allay her anxiety. She telephoned Janet at the Whately Hall and then, leaving Fanny in charge, hurried across to Norham Road to tell Doreen. They decided there was nothing they could do but write him a letter and hope to see him soon. She told Doreen about the incident with Fanny and the cooker.

"I expect she's like Dad, a bit short-tempered. Best to take no notice."

"I know I need help but I won't put up with too much of her nonsense," said Louie, walking to the door. "I'd better get back to see what she's up to."

Doreen watched her hurrying down the road and felt uneasy about Fanny's behaviour. She decided to go over to Number Ten that evening to reassure herself that all was well.

Louie returned home and on entering the kitchen could not believe her eyes, the cooker was being subjected to another good scouring.

"I've nearly finished," Fanny was smiling, "I've done the cupboards."

Louie's heart sank when she saw the dismantled cooker. It was time to cook dinner and she wondered how long it would take to assemble it this time. She just said, "Well done," and retreated to another room, desperately anxious not to upset Fanny again. She waited as long as she dared, opened the kitchen door and peeped inside to see the last pieces of the cooker being slotted into place. With a sigh of relief she started to prepare the meal only to be interrupted by the sound of raised voices coming from the dining room. She hurried to the scene to find Fanny, very red in the face, screaming abuse at the daily help who was close to tears.

"I always lay the tables, don't I Mrs Hutt?" she cried.

"Yes, please carry on." Louie hustled Fanny from the room and was about to tell her she must leave her employ when she turned and fled up the stairs, so Louie returned to the dining room to pacify Monica, the unhappy daily help.

Louie's mind was made up, she could stand Fanny's tantrums no longer, so later that evening she called her into her private room to dismiss her. When she appeared she was in tears and seemed genuinely sorry for her behaviour. She begged Louie to forgive her and Louie was persuaded, against her better judgement, to let her stay on. When Doreen arrived Louie told her what had happened and confided in her that her life was fraught with anxiety waiting for Fanny's next outburst.

A telegram from Don took her mind off her domestic worries, it just said: COMING HOME. LOVE DON. She knew how the brothers would be missing each other and wished that Wilf could have come home too. While he was stationed in Germany he had joined a motorcycle club. A few young soldiers gathered together to make up machines out of old discarded army models. Wilf built himself a racing motorcycle and was enjoying great success out there. Jack had bought a very fast DKW and attended all the local race meetings. Some aerodromes, now disused, made ideal race tracks. One such, was at Haddenham not far from Thame and only a stone's throw from Oxford, so Jack was a frequent competitor there.

When Don came home on sick leave to recuperate, he was in his element tinkering with Jack's machines and it was not long before he too had acquired a motorcycle and joined Jack on the race tracks and was obviously enjoying himself. Louie was pleased for him, she reasoned that if he could beat such a deadly disease as meningitis "lady luck" must be on his side.

She even watched him race a couple of times but the noise of the machines revving up in the paddock gave her such a headache that she opted out to stay at home with Sylvia. It was not long, however, before Don was well enough to return to his unit and had to leave his beloved motorcycle behind.

Jack became more ambitious and travelled farther afield, sometimes as far as Cadwell Park in Lincolnshire, a racetrack that was becoming very popular with the top riders. It was set in a hollow surrounded with grassy banks which served as a natural grandstand. Doreen and Jack would set off in the Jaguar at an unearthly hour in the morning with the DKW perched precariously on a trailer that Jack had managed to acquire cheaply. The car boot was loaded with his leathers and tools, also plenty of sandwiches and home-made fruit cake. He had cut the side out of a large square biscuit tin which acted as a wind shield for the Primus stove to provide boiling water for an outsize teapot.

Jack's Jag soon became a popular meeting place with the riders and their families. John Surtees was about ten years old, his father raced a motorcycle and sidecar. With his passenger or sidecar man, who with skill and daring bobbed from side to side to balance the machine, they were rarely beaten and young John helped as general dogsbody. Doreen admired the dedication of the lad and enjoyed their little chats over cups of tea. She felt sure he would some day be a champion himself and her prediction proved to be correct.

The handsome Geoff Duke was popular with the riders in spite of the fact that when he was in a race they did not stand much chance of being first to the chequered flag. He was a brilliant rider and Jack was really happy if he could finish second to Geoff. He would laughingly quote the saying: "it's not so much the winning as the taking part", but winning was really what it was all about.

Doreen and Jack were away at a motorcycle race meeting. Sylvia was staying with Louie so they decided to take a picnic into the park. They found a pleasant spot under a tree, spread a blanket on the grass and were enjoying their sandwiches when Sylvia spotted a gentleman walking towards them.

"Isn't that Mr Sloane?" she asked.

"Yes you're right. He's seen us. Look, he's waving."

"How lovely to see you," Henry Sloane was smiling broadly. "You both look well and hasn't Sylvia grown."

He seemed genuinely pleased to meet them and while Sylvia wandered off to play he sat down for a chat. He told Louie that although Mildred quite liked her new home she found it a very tiring house to run in spite of having a daily cleaner and a gardener. "Of course I still like to potter in the garden. I often recollect the happy hours we spent together in your garden, Louie. I so enjoyed your company." He had moved closer to her and was gazing into her eyes.

Louie glanced at her watch. "My goodness, is that the time? I should have been home ages ago." She jumped up and hastily packed up the picnic things. "Come on Sylvia, we must get back."

"It's been so nice to see you, Louie. Perhaps we might meet again?" said Henry.

"Yes, that would be nice," she replied as she handed Sylvia a basket to carry and they hurried away.

Louie felt uneasy about her meeting with Henry. He had always had an amiable manner, which she had taken to be innocent friendship. Today, however, he seemed overly friendly and she hoped he did not mean anything more serious. There was no way that she was going to get involved with a married man. She decided not to walk in the parks for a while so as to avoid meeting him.

Louie was still having trouble with Fanny. While Don was at home she was quite well-behaved but as soon as he returned to his unit she started playing up and losing her temper. She was quite obsessed with the cooker and Louie had to be extra careful not to spill any food for fear of her flying off the handle. Doreen noticed her mother was looking tired and suggested she take a short holiday. It was then that Louie admitted she was at the end of her tether.

"How can I leave her?" she said. "I hardly dare go to the shops in case she picks a quarrel with someone and I'm half afraid to go into my own kitchen."

"You can't go on like this," said Doreen. "Something must be done."

"I had years of your father's tantrums but I was married to him."

"Well you're not married to Fanny and the sooner you get rid of her the better!"

"I'll do it today and I won't let her get round me this time. In fact, I've been thinking of making a fresh start altogether as the lease on Number Ten runs out soon. Mr

Rose has advised me to look for a house to buy and leave Bradmore Road. I'll ask the guests to find other accommodation, have a week or two at the seaside, then look for a new home."

"What a good idea. Perhaps you could find a more modern house that's easier to run?" said Doreen. "Maybe a different way of heating the bath water?"

Louie laughed, the gas geezer in the bathroom was very efficient but you had to be careful how you lit it, as Wilf found to his cost one day, when he turned it on and took a little while to find his cigarette lighter. There was the most almighty bang when he gave the lighter a flick and the next day they found it in the garden. Luckily Wilf was not hurt, just a little deaf for a few days. "No more gas geezers, but I shall miss the old place, we've had some happy times there as well as some sad ones."

Most of Louie's guests were only staying on a temporary basis, so asking them to leave was not going to be a problem. Mrs Slesenger had returned to America. Jane and Olive, however, had been such loyal guests and friends that Louie was worried as to how she was going to broach the subject. When she told Olive her plans she was surprised that her reaction was laughter.

"Jane and I were wondering how to tell you that we'll be moving. I've decided to buy a little house that has come up for sale near The Cedars and Jane is coming to live with me. Even when the servicemen have moved on we thought we could still be of some help to the other patients. We don't seem to have had much luck in the marriage stakes and are glad of each other's company."

There was a tearful scene and much begging and pleading but this time Louie stood her ground and Fanny left at the end of her month's notice to everyone's relief and Louie's kitchen was hers once more, cooker and all.

"I think I'll go to Barmouth, I like Wales," she said when the last of the guests had departed. "Simmy says she would love to come with me so I'm very much looking forward to it."

CHAPTER
NINE

Doreen had a new paying guest, George Ross. He had been a physical training instructor in the army but now had an administrative position in a firm that produced Biro pens. This new ball-point pen had just been invented and was very much the "in thing" though many said it would never replace the traditional fountain pen. He soon made himself at home and, in his quiet way, got on well with the other guests. Janet met him on one of her visits to Norham Road, after which she seemed to call quite frequently. It had undoubtedly been love at first sight for both of them and it was not long before Janet came to show her sister a very beautiful engagement ring and announced that she was to become Mrs George Ross. Doreen was so pleased for her and was soon helping her with her wedding plans. After Algy's death each of his children received a share of his estate so Janet decided to buy a house and take in paying guests as she had had plenty of experience helping her mother. When a large house became available, close to the centre of Oxford on the Iffley Road, it seemed ideal, so she bought it without hesitation.

"George is complaining of a bad back," Doreen told Jack one evening.

"Why don't you offer to rub it with some of the embrocation you brought back from your father's farm?"

"He might not like me to, you know how it stinks. Anyway, I don't know whether it's for use on humans or animals, but I suppose I could ask him if he'd like to try it," Doreen replied as she headed for the stairs. "He thinks he's a little better," she told Jack when she returned, "but he doesn't look too good to me. There are only two weeks to go before the wedding, I just hope he'll be better by then."

The smell of embrocation wafted through the house as Doreen set to work rubbing George's back at every opportunity and after a week his condition had improved and thankfully he was up and about in time for the big day.

The morning of the wedding Sylvia rose bright and early only to discover that she was covered in large itchy spots and it did not take the doctor long to confirm that she had chickenpox. The West family would not be joining in the wedding celebrations and disappointed though Sylvia was she consoled herself with the fact that she would not be going to school for a while. Edith and Jacky travelled up from Weston-super-Mare. Edith, who looked lovely as Maid of Honour, lent Janet her beautiful white wedding gown, which fitted her perfectly. The bride also wore a blue garter, so, wearing something borrowed and something blue, she was sure her marriage was to bring good luck and happiness.

After a short honeymoon the happy couple moved into their new home on the Iffley Road. A few weeks later

Janet telephoned Doreen to say that George was not well and his doctor had sent him to the Radcliffe Infirmary to see a specialist. The next day he had to return for further tests and when the doctor took Janet into his consulting room for a quiet talk the bottom fell out of her world. He told her that her beloved George had cancer and took some time to explain the seriousness of his condition. When she finally left she walked down the long gloomy corridors and out into the sunshine where a fountain was playing in front of the hospital. The sun shone on the droplets of water as they sprayed high into the air falling like teardrops. She wiped away her own tears and walked through the huge iron gates into the street. She headed towards Norham Road hoping that Doreen would be at home, she needed to share her troubles with someone. She found Doreen working in the kitchen and they talked and cried together. Later in the afternoon they went to tell their mother the sad news. Louie was in her lounge covering the furniture with dust sheets, the last of her guests had left and she was preparing for her holiday.

"Mother looks very tired, don't you think?" said Janet when Doreen was walking back with her to the hospital.

"Yes, I'm hoping a week or two of rest and sea air will do her good. I'm glad Simmy is going with her, they get on so well. Vera is joining them later, then she'll bring them home in her car."

Louie had sold Algy's Wolseley, she really did not have the use for it now that she lived in town and she no longer had Babs to drive her, besides, Doreen lived so near and would take her anywhere in her car. She had planned with Simmy to travel to Barmouth by train, they were to leave bright and early the next morning. Doreen took them to the station and waved goodbye until the train was out of sight.

Jack was preparing for a trip to a race meeting at Cadwell Park. He was going to pick up two pals on the way, Jim Goldby from Adderbury and Maurice Musselwhite from Faringdon. Doreen decided to stay at home with Sylvia. She filled a hamper with all the goodies she could muster plus the faithful Primus stove. At four o'clock next morning they kissed goodbye and she watched the DKW, shining in all its glory, being towed away.

She set about her chores and soon had the house looking spick-and-span, determined to spend a happy day with Sylvia, who had just come down for breakfast.

"You choose where we go," she said, but guessed what the answer would be.

Sylvia loved animals so it was no surprise to Doreen that her immediate response was, "Could we go to the zoo?"

"Hurry up and eat your breakfast then, it's quite a long way."

They were soon heading out of Oxford towards Dunstable Downs where they stopped to stretch their legs and look at the view. There were not many people about, the sun was shining and there was a cool breeze which had encouraged a few families with children to bring their kites. The rolling downs made an ideal place to fly them from and Doreen and Sylvia were fascinated watching them, sometimes so high and sometimes plummeting to the ground. They lost track of time and decided they must hurry if they wanted to spend time at the zoo. So it was off to Whipsnade to enjoy a glorious afternoon looking at the many species of animals until pangs of hunger told them it was time to make tracks for home. When they returned to the little Austin, they found it had a very flat tyre.

"How could you do this to me?" Doreen remonstrated as she searched for the tools and the rather bald spare tyre. It did not take long to change the wheel but she fervently hoped they would not get another puncture on the way home and breathed a sigh of relief when they reached Norham Road in time to cook supper for the guests.

Jack arrived home at midnight tired but in high spirits having won a race so, all in all, it had been quite a day. He slept little that night in spite of being so tired. His win had fired him with enthusiasm and plans to enter the Manx Grand Prix were taking shape in his mind. By the time he eventually fell asleep it was only to dream that he was in the Isle of Man racing his motorcycle along those narrow roads, but Doreen woke him with a cup of tea before he reached the finish.

"Come on! Alfie's on the phone, you're needed at the garage."

"Now I'll never know if I'd have won," he murmured to himself and decided that a trip to the Isle of Man was next on the agenda.

* * *

Louie and Simmy were really enjoying themselves in Barmouth and when Vera went down to join them she found them sitting in deck chairs on the beach knitting socks. Neither of them were very proficient in the art of knitting but with wartime shortages they had mastered socks and gloves, often having to unpick old garments to get enough wool. Vera was pleased to see they had benefited from the rest and sea air. They both had pale complexions, but sported a hint of colour in their cheeks. *I don't think it's rouge*, she thought whilst attempting to set up a deck chair for herself, then finally giving up. "It's no good," she said and sank down onto the warm sands. "I never could make them stand up."

Simmy laughed and handed her her knitting, "I'm not much good at turning the heel, so you can do that for me while I sort out your deck chair, exchange is no robbery." No sooner had she made the wretched chair stand firmly on the sand than the deck chair attendant appeared to claim his dues.

"Don't pay him for mine," Vera joked, "I haven't sat in it yet."

Over dinner that evening Louie told them of her plan to buy a house and give up Number Ten.

"Doreen will miss you," said Vera.

"I'm not going to move too far away. I'm afraid Janet will be needing help in a while. With George so poorly she'll want her family near. There's a house on the Woodstock Road I've got my eye on but I haven't made up my mind yet."

The weather was so lovely they decided to stay on for another week and explored the local countryside in

Vera's car. The scenery was breathtaking and they found several small coves that were practically deserted. Bikinis had come into fashion and if you had a half-decent figure they replaced the all in one bathing costume. Vera sported a pretty pink one and after a swim would lie on the beach and sunbathe while Louie and Simmy paddled with their frocks tucked into their knickers. They were all loath to leave Barmouth, though Louie and Simmy were secretly getting a little homesick. When, after a long drive home, Vera pulled up in Bradmore Road, Louie was glad to be back and wondered if she was doing the right thing to move from there especially when she saw Sylvia running out to meet them. She had obviously been watching for their car.

Louie had employed a Polish girl called Eileen after Fanny left and she had kept house while she was away. When they entered the house everywhere was spotless and all the furniture shone. Eileen was quite alone in the world, both her parents were killed in the war. She was a bright little girl and a good worker. Having lost all her possessions she was reluctant to throw anything away. Since coming to England she had saved everything she could lay her hands on. It was all carefully folded and stowed away. She showed Doreen inside her wardrobe which was full to the brim of little strips of material and old clothes, washed and ironed and draped on hangers that she had padded and decorated.

"Now the war is over," she said in broken English, "I shall return to Poland when I have saved enough money." Doreen wondered if she intended to take all her hoardings with her and how many suitcases she would need.

Louie and Doreen were having a quiet chat one evening. Jack had gone for a drink with his pals, so it was an opportunity for Doreen to broach the subject of their plans to go to the Isle of Man. She knew that Louie would be worried about Jack racing there as it was such a dangerous course. A few of their friends were going to join them including Maurice Musselwhite and his wife Mary and Jim Golby and his wife Ann. They were all booked to stay at the same hotel. Donald and Wilfred hoped to get leave and travel over as soon as they could get away. Sylvia was determined to go though Doreen was worried that she might not enjoy the journey and hoped the weather would be kind to them.

"Won't you come with us, Mother?" she said.

"I suppose I could have come now that I don't have any guests to cater for," said Louie. "But I may be moving house by then so it's difficult to make plans, though I shall worry all the time you're away."

"Have you thought any more about the house on the Woodstock Road?" Doreen asked.

"Yes, but I don't think it's right for me. I'm going to look at a few more houses before I make up my mind."

There was a month to go before the trip to The Island and Norham Road was a hive of industry, so much to get ready. Jack was working at the garage making preparations for his absence and preparing his DKW motorcycle for the big event, stripping, rebuilding its engine and tuning it to perfection. He would work all hours until it was just right. The DKW had an exhaust note unlike any other motorcycle, a very high pitched sound which meant taking it into the country to test it, not wishing to upset the neighbours.

Finally, the day for their departure had arrived. It meant a very early start to journey to Liverpool in time to catch the ferry to the Isle of Man. They could not travel very fast towing the motorcycle on the little trailer and when they reached the Mersey Tunnel on the outskirts of Liverpool the traffic was held up at the entrance as someone had broken down inside and had to be towed away. They did not have to wait long, however, and were soon travelling through the eerie subway. They were thankful when they emerged out of the darkness at the other end. They reached the docks just in time to load the car and motorcycle aboard the ferry and Doreen watched anxiously as Jack drove up a very narrow ramp.

The clouds were gathering and the wind and rain made it unpleasant for the men loading the many motorcycles. Doreen and Sylvia joined the other passengers as they hurried to go aboard out of the rain. Jack was waiting at the top of the gangway and took them below for some welcome refreshment. However, the boat had barely left the quayside before he was making a hasty exit towards the Gents and Sylvia too was complaining that she felt sick. Doreen, though hating the rough voyage, was not plagued with sea sickness so was able to keep an eye on them. After about an hour, as Jack stood on deck, clinging to the rail and looking like death warmed-up, a passing sailor stopped to ask him if he was all right.

"You'll soon feel better," he said. "It's all to do with the tides. When we get past 'The Irish Rapids' things will calm down." Jack thanked him for his reassurance. Looking out over the angry sea, he paid little heed to his prediction. However, not more than ten minutes had passed before his sickness had gone.

Don and Wilf and their friends travelled over the next day. The weather had not let up and their crossing was not a pleasant one but, by the following morning, in time for the practice, the sun put in an appearance so the women headed for the beach while the men went off to meet and chat with the riders who were tuning their engines between practice runs.

After dinner they all went to the cinema to see the famous film shown every year starring George Formby as a rider in the TT races, there were screams of laughter as he performed his antics. Then, to round off a thoroughly enjoyable evening they walked along the promenade eating fish and chips out of newspaper.

Jack's race took place the next day. They were awakened by the deafening sound of motorcycles revving under their bedroom window, spectators roaring off to find the best vantage points to watch the race. Jack's supporters chose to sit in the stands where they were more or less kept informed of the riders' progress.

There was no mistaking the sound of the DKW when Jack's turn came on the starting grid and when he had completed the first lap well up with the leaders excitement grew among his supporters, but on the third lap he failed to appear.

"Shouldn't we have seen Jack by now?" Doreen asked Maurice.

"I expect he'll be along soon," he said, not wanting to alarm her.

A few minutes later the commentator's voice came over the loudspeaker, "Number six seems to have gone missing."

Doreen's heart sank. "Where can he be? They must know where he is!"

"Don't worry they'll find him." Wilf was by her side. "He's probably broken down."

"But they would have seen him if he had. Why haven't they found him?" The minutes passed and still no mention.

Sylvia by this time was asking where Daddy was and before her mother could answer a voice over the loudspeaker blared out loud and clear, "Number six has been spotted on the far side of the course. He's safe but appears to have broken down."

"Never mind, there's always next year," said Don.

"I'm just relieved that he's all right," gasped Doreen. "At least he put up a good show and I bet he enjoyed himself."

They settled down to watch the rest of the race which ended in thrilling fashion as two riders raced neck and neck to the chequered flag. There had been quite a few tumbles and breakdowns but no one had been badly injured. About an hour later a weary figure appeared on the horizon pushing his motorcycle and Wilf and Don ran to help him. As he drew near Doreen could see that beneath its covering of oil and grime his face was aglow, he'd had the thrill of his life.

The next day was spent exploring the lovely island. Ramsay was a delight, they all loved it and were loath to move on but there was so much to see. On to Laxey with its famous wheel, where they were fortunate to be able to buy some wool which was scarce on the mainland. A shop near the bay sold the famous Manx kippers which could be bought packed in boxes and dispatched anywhere in the United Kingdom. A tasty gift, though a little unusual, Doreen spent the last of her holiday money sending boxes home to all her friends. They completed their trip with a ride round the race track which had been opened to the public. Churchtown, Kate's Cottage, Kirk Michael and Creg-ny-Baa had all become famous landmarks on the course. They returned to Douglas where they relaxed, playing on the sands with Sylvia until it was time for dinner.

"I wish we could stay another week, there's so much to see and do," said Doreen as they took their seats at the dinner table. "It's so nice to be waited on for a change."

"Well, we'll be back next year," promised Jack.

After an excellent meal the rest of the party went out for a final drink but Doreen sat in the lounge with Sylvia where they were soon joined by the proprietress. She told them that she and her husband had only been living in the Isle of Man for a short time. Their home was in Liverpool when the war ended and when they were demobbed they decided they would like to run a hotel. When The Crest came up for sale they thought it would be ideal and the extra visitors for the TT races were an added bonus. Doreen asked her if she felt cut-off living on such a small island.

"When I first came I didn't think I'd be able to go on living here," she said. "I'd sit and look out at the sea and break my heart. Tom, my husband, never knew. I've come to terms with it now and grown fond of the island. In this business I meet so many interesting people that I never get the chance to feel lonely."

Doreen told her that she and her mother ran guest houses in Oxford and they exchanged tales of some of their unusual guests. There was so much to talk about, it was as if they had known each other all their lives. It seemed no time at all before the others returned, a little inebriated, tired, but happy and Doreen followed her new friend Maggy to the kitchen to help with the cocoa and biscuits. As they sat in the bay window supping their bedtime drink and gazing at the wonderful sunset, like a ball of fire on the horizon, Doreen hoped it was a good omen for tomorrow's weather and promised a better crossing.

Sure enough, they woke next morning to bright sunshine and the sea looked as smooth as a duck pond with hardly a ripple. They left the hotel and collected their cars and motorcycles to assemble on the docks.

The voyage was delightful especially as Don and Wilf were able to travel with them. Together with their friends they all sat down to a meal of Manx kippers with thick slices of bread and butter, washed down with glasses of Guinness.

CHAPTER
TEN

On their return from the Isle of Man there was so much to do, but first a visit to Iffley Road to see Janet and George. Sylvia ran up the steps to their front door, she couldn't wait to see them again. Janet looked tired and George pale but he did not seem to be in any pain. They were relieved to know that Jack was safe as an article had appeared in the *Oxford Mail* with the heading: "OXFORD MAN MISSING ON TT COURSE". It had named the missing rider as Jack West but failed to report whether he had been found safe.

Doreen and Sylvia called on Louie on the way home, she had just received the particulars of a house so they arranged to view it that afternoon. It was not until Louie was getting into the car that she mentioned that the house was in Reading. Doreen was surprised. She didn't say anything, started the car and headed off out of Oxford. Sylvia was chatting away to her Granny and it was not until they had nearly reached Reading that Doreen asked Louie why they were looking at a house in this area, but Louie would not be drawn.

"It's only taken an hour to get here," she said.

"But why Reading?" Doreen repeated.

"Well property is less expensive. I can't find a house I like in Oxford."

They finally located the house and were shown inside. The interior was gloomy and in need of refurbishment. The only thing in its favour was a large conservatory which led into the tiny garden. So when, as they walked to the car, Louie said, "this'll do me well," Doreen could hardly believe her ears.

"Did you really like it?" she ventured.

"Not a lot, but it's better than the ones I've seen so far and it's cheap. If Mr Rose thinks it's all right I shall make them an offer."

On the way home Doreen stopped at the Shillingford Bridge Hotel. "Let's have some tea," she said. The weather was pleasantly warm so they sat in the garden near to the river.

"This is nice," said Louie when a waiter brought tea and cakes. Doreen hoped she would relax and tell her why she wanted to move so far away. After tea they strolled along the towpath before heading for home and still Louie remained unusually quiet.

Doreen told Jack that evening about the day's happenings and how worried she was for her mother, especially as Don and Wilf were not due to leave the army for another six months, so Louie would be living alone if she went ahead with the Reading house. It was unlikely that Janet would be able to visit her very often as George's health had deteriorated and he was going to need more nursing.

"Even if she goes," he said, "I bet she'll be back in less than a year."

Louie's offer was accepted and within a month she moved to Reading. Doreen helped her pack with a heavy heart and as the pantechnicon moved off they had a last look round before following in the car. As they walked from room to room memories flooded back and Louie felt a lump in her throat.

"Penny for your thoughts. You were miles away," said Doreen.

"I suppose I really will be soon, but it may not be for long and thank goodness for the telephone. I know you'll visit me as often as you can."

"Of course we will."

"I've made up my mind to make a fresh start. This is as good a place as any," said Louie as they drove through the outskirts of Reading.

When they reached the house the men were already unloading the furniture. "It won't take me long to get straight," she said. "It'll look better when I've hung the curtains and unpacked the ornaments and pictures."

Doreen made her way back to Oxford unhappy about leaving her mother so alone. As she turned into Norham Road she noticed a man who looked familiar, walking along the pavement on the other side of the road, and a second glance confirmed that it was Henry Sloane. Curiosity got the better of her and, after parking the car in her drive, she walked to the corner where she could see the length of Bradmore Road. He had stopped outside Number Ten and was staring at the house.

"Hello Henry," she called out as she drew nearer to him. "Can I help you?"

"Oh, hello Doreen," he seemed agitated. "I was wondering if Louie is all right. The house looks so deserted."

"She's fine," Doreen reassured him. "She's just moved house today. She's gone to live in Reading."

"Oh dear. I'd like to keep in touch with her. She's been such a good friend to me."

Doreen was puzzled, Louie had told her that Henry was no more than just another paying guest. "Don't worry. I'll let you have her new address," she said.

She wondered whether Henry had anything to do with Louie's departure and that evening she told Jack what had happened.

"Do you think your mother's having an affair?" he said with a mischievous grin.

"Well, she would hardly take herself off thirty miles away if she was."

"Whatever it is, you can be sure she'll sort it out," Jack sounded confident. "Louie's a very resourceful lady."

Meanwhile, in Reading, the removal men had gone leaving Louie alone in her new home. She wandered from room to room, it was all so drab. She was near to tears. *Pull yourself together, Louie,* she thought. *It might not be so bad with a lick of paint.*

After buying the Reading house and the expense of moving Louie realized that she had spent more than anticipated. Mr Rose's advice to buy a house made sense, but after the children had had their share of the estate and some of the money was to be held in trust for them, it left precious little for Louie to live on. She was going to have to economize.

The next day she found a handy store and newsagent and bought enough food to stock her larder and a local

114

newspaper. After scanning the columns to find a decorator she contacted a cheerful young man whose rates seemed reasonable but he would not be able to start work on her house for a month. *What am I going to do with myself stuck in this dreariness for a month?* She searched through the advertisements and found a cheap second-hand bicycle. Now she would be able to take trips into town or countryside without the expense of running a car.

A week later Olive telephoned, "I know it's a bit soon after your move but could we bring a couple of the boys over for a cup of tea? We're dying to see your new house."

Louie was delighted, "It'll be lovely to see you all, though I'm still in a muddle. I can't finish unpacking until the decorating is done."

She hurriedly baked a cake and made sandwiches. The Daimler purred to a halt in the driveway with Jane at the wheel. Louie ran out to welcome them and they helped the two young men inside. One was on crutches and the other had a patch over one eye and was a little shaky on his feet. They were obviously taken aback when they saw the house, it was very different from the elegance of Number Ten. However, a good time was had by all and the dreary house was soon filled with laughter.

The lads seemed to enjoy their outing so when it was time for them to leave Louie asked Olive if they would like to bring more of their boys on regular visits, perhaps every fortnight? Olive said she thought it was a wonderful idea. "Give us all something to look forward to and do the car good to have a decent run," she said.

"By the way, Jane, it's my turn to drive home." Louie laughed as they drove off. Now she had something to plan for and she was determined to make the house more presentable though it was going to take time.

When Tony, the decorator, started work, Louie knew that she had found a "treasure". He was always cheerful, careful not to leave a mess and tactfully suggested just the right wallpapers and colours to brighten the rooms. She had plenty of curtains and floor coverings from Home Farm and Number Ten and pretty soon the house had taken on a new lease of life.

The conservatory still needed renovation but Louie decided to tackle that herself. She scoured the old glass panes, rubbed down the woodwork and painted it white. When all the rubbish had been cleared out it was quite spacious. With comfortable chairs and some attractive plants it was going to be a pleasant place to sit and relax. The nearest garden nursery was about three miles away, so she pedalled off on her old bike to see what goodies she could find. She wobbled home with her basket filled with plants. It took several trips but she soon had the conservatory alive with greenery, some of the flowers already in bloom.

Now that the house was shipshape, Louie decided that she had earned a little holiday so she telephoned Doreen to see if Sylvia might like to join her for a few days by the sea as she knew that she had another week left of her school holiday before term started. Sylvia was thrilled at the idea, she loved her Granny dearly and missed popping round to Bradmore Road. Doreen took her to

Reading that afternoon, they spent a happy time planning where to go, finally deciding on Margate. They were to travel by train, so two days later Doreen waved goodbye to them from the platform at Reading station, Sylvia proudly carrying her very own new red suitcase bought specially for the occasion.

The house seemed very quiet without her, so when Jack suggested taking his motorcycle to Cadwell Park at the weekend Doreen readily agreed. He had not raced it since the Manx TT and was hoping he had rectified the engine trouble.

"I think it would be a good idea if we go up the day before and stay the night," said Doreen. She knew after such a long journey Jack would find it difficult to concentrate on his racing and he frequently suffered from headaches. Mr Stamford knew that area well and recommended a comfortable inn quite near to Cadwell Park. Doreen telephoned and booked a room and they set off the next day arriving in the late afternoon.

"It doesn't look much of a place," said Jack as they drove into the tiny car park. The inn looked very dilapidated but Doreen thought that as Mr Stamford had recommended it it must be all right.

They were welcomed by the landlord who led them through a poky little bar and up some narrow winding stairs to their bedroom. The whole place smelt frowsty.

Doreen threw open the window. "I just can't believe Mr Stamford would recommend this."

Jack sat on the bed, it was as hard as a board. There was a wash basin but when Doreen turned on the hot tap a strange gurgling noise produced a few drops of water, then nothing. She tried the cold one and only a slow trickle emerged.

I suppose we'll have to stay now, it's too late to find another room anywhere else," she said. "At least the bed linen looks clean." The motorcycle race meetings were so popular that while they were being held the hotels were full to overflowing for miles around. They crept into their hard bed and twisted and turned to avoid lying on the lumps but were so tired after their long journey they soon fell asleep.

They awoke next morning to the strong smell of fried bacon and were soon sitting down to a hearty breakfast served in the bar. The landlord and his wife joined them for a chat and to wish Jack good luck, then they were on their way to Cadwell Park.

When they arrived and drove into the paddock young John Surtees came running over to say hello and was soon helping Jack to unload his motorcycle. Maurice and Mary Musselwhite were next to arrive, then Jim and Ann Golby. Jack told them about their uncomfortable bed and there were hoots of laughter.

"Good thing it wasn't your honeymoon, Doreen," said Maurice with a saucy grin.

The day went well and Jack was more than satisfied with his motorcycle, happy to be third in the race. At least the engine had not let him down this time. The kettle on the Primus in the biscuit tin was working overtime and many cups of tea were consumed before the long trek home.

The following morning Mr Stamford tapped on the kitchen door to ask about their trip, he seemed very curious to know what their accommodation was like and before Doreen could answer, apologized, explaining that it was not until after they had left that he realized that he had given them the wrong name for the inn.

"Never mind," said Doreen. "It wasn't too bad. They were nice people and we had a good breakfast." She omitted to tell him about the lumpy bed.

On the corner of Norham Road and Banbury Road stood a hotel called The Cotswold Lodge and when Doreen was away her guests would go there for their meals. Mr Stamford told her that he had become quite friendly with the proprietor who was hoping to convert a loft over his garages into a flat. Knowing that he was an architect, he had asked his advice.

"I told him I would be pleased to help," he said, "and if it was to be let I'd like first option as a prospective tenant. I don't expect he'll be able to get planning permission but it would be nice."

Doreen agreed, "It would be ideal and you could design it to suit yourself." She knew, however, she would be sorry to see him go.

Louie and Sylvia had returned from Margate and Jack and Doreen travelled to Reading to collect Sylvia. It was obvious the holiday had been a great success. Louie was looking so much better, the sea air and rest had worked miracles and they couldn't stop talking about it. The weather had been lovely and they had spent most of the time on the sands, Louie relaxed in her deck chair with a book while Sylvia played with the other children and rode on the donkeys.

CHAPTER
ELEVEN

Six months later planning permission was granted for the flat at The Cotswold Lodge and Mr Stamford set about designing and overseeing the work on what was to be his new home. When it was finished and he had moved in, Doreen, Jack and Sylvia were first to be invited to tea. It was a beautiful flat and he was very proud of it.

"It must be nice not to have to share the bathroom," remarked Doreen. "There always seems to be a queue."

"That's true, but I miss your cooking and I hate washing-up," he said. "I had no idea that shopping for one would be so time consuming."

Don and Wilf were now living with their mother in Reading, having completed their National Service. Christmas was drawing near and Louie had invited Olive and Jane and some of their boys to spend Christmas day with her and her boys. Olive said that they could squeeze three lads into the Daimler and Wilf offered to collect the other two in the little sports car that he had just bought.

Louie draped the house with Christmas decorations and when she stood back and surveyed her work she had to admit that she was pleased with the transformation. Among all her lovely Christmas cards, one puzzled her slightly. It was from Mildred and Henry with an extra note wishing her happiness in her new home. She was sure it was in Henry's handwriting, but how did he know her address?

The boys all got on well together, laughing and joking and they described Louie's lunch as a feast fit for a king. Later, as they relaxed in the lounge, Olive sat quietly observing every detail of the room. "You've done a wonderful job on this house, Louie," she said. "I'm sure if you put it on the market now you'd make a considerable profit. I think you should move. With your talents you could always earn some money by improving old houses and selling them on." There was a hush in the room as her remarks took everyone by surprise.

"Now that Louie is so comfortable here she might not want to move," said Jane tactfully. She knew that at times Olive could be too outspoken.

"Well I think it's a good idea," said Louie. "I'll telephone the local estate agents tomorrow and get the house valued."

Don laughed, "Now look what you've done, Olive. We'll never get Mother to settle down."

Later that evening, when her guests had gone and she was sitting quietly looking at the lovely plant that the boys from The Cedars had given her, Louie had time to think about what Olive had said. It might be just the answer she was looking for to solve her money problems.

After a valuation, it was obvious that she would indeed make a sizeable profit on the house and the local estate agent said that he thought he could soon find a buyer. This proved to be true, so Louie had to find herself a new home.

She telephoned John Brooks, an Oxford estate agent, and after a friendly chat, he recommended a property on Cumnor Hill called Clanfield that he thought might suit her. Wilf was not surprised when she asked him to take her to see a house in Oxford. He was pleased to oblige as neither of the boys felt at home in Reading.

They set off, Wilf taking care to moderate his speed for Louie's sake. After a few miles, as they drove gently through the countryside, she began to fidget. "Not very fast for a sports car, Wilf. Is this the best it can do?" He accelerated away and they reached Cumnor Hill in no time.

Clanfield was a most attractive house and, after a quick inspection, Louie had fallen in love with it. They made their way to Norham Road to talk it over with Doreen and telephone Mr Rose. He soon put the wheels in motion and in a short while Louie was back in Oxford to the delight of her family.

She decided to get two of the bedrooms decorated before putting the carpets down, so told the removal men to leave a divan in the dining room where she would sleep until the work was completed. Don and Wilf were away for the weekend helping Jack at a motorcycle meeting, so Louie was alone in the house. She was quite used to being on her own and happily went to bed early. She was tired after the move and soon fell fast asleep.

She was awakened with a start. There was a noise under her bed! She lay still in the pitch darkness, hardly daring to breathe listening to strange rustling and scraping noises which seemed to come from all around the room. Then, just as a cloud had passed to reveal the moon, which shone brightly, something landed with a thud on Louie's bed. She found herself staring into the eyes of the largest, blackest cat she had ever seen and it was standing firmly on her legs. The fan light was open but she wondered how a cat that size could have squeezed through. She thought it must have belonged to the previous owners and been desperate to return. Her heart still thumping, she got out of bed and gently lifted the frightened cat to carry it to the kitchen as the grandfather clock struck three. She made herself a cup of tea and gave the intruder a saucer of milk which it drank with gusto.

Louie could not get to sleep again so rose early to do some gardening before breakfast. She telephoned the previous owners of Clanfield who were relieved to know that their cat was safe but amazed that it had come so far, as their new home was at least ten miles away. They were soon ringing the doorbell and reunited with their wandering "moggy".

"It may be an old wives' tale, but you could try buttering her paws," Louie suggested. "It's supposed to settle them down."

The following morning Louie opened her door to bring in the milk and was surprised to find a bunch of flowers on her doorstep. There was a label attached which read: "WELCOME BACK TO OXFORD. BEST

WISHES, HENRY." For a moment it took her breath away. She was unhappy that he seemed to know her every move. However, a telephone call to Doreen later in the day solved the mystery.

"I met Henry in the park last week and he asked after you. I didn't think you'd mind if I told him that you were moving again," she said.

"No. Of course I don't mind." Louie realized that it was just a coincidence that Henry had learnt of her move and that the flowers were a very kind gesture.

The boys returned from their trip with Jack and after watching him compete were more keen than ever to get back on the race track themselves. After a hasty lunch they retreated to the garage to work on their machines leaving Louie on her own to do the washing up.

She heard a ring at the front door, quickly dried her hands, and was delighted to find Simmy on the doorstep. She soon put the kettle on and over a cup of tea they caught up on all the news. Louie couldn't wait to show her round her new home, for which she was full of admiration. She had given up her own home and gone to live with Vera, who now had a large comfortable house on the Botley Road which she ran as a guest house.

"The boys are hell bent on riding in the Manx TT races this year," Louie told Simmy. "I expect Jack and Doreen will be going too. I think I'd like to go and watch them. Better to know what's going on than to stay at home and worry and I've never been to the Isle of Man. I don't suppose you'd like to come?"

"I'd love to come. I've heard it's a lovely island, what fun we shall have!"

The weeks flew by and it was time to set sail for "The Island". Doreen was not able to leave the guest house and was pleased that Simmy was joining Louie for the trip. She knew that Jack would have plenty of help from his friends. The excitement mounted as the final preparations were completed on the racing machines, everything had to be carefully checked from their leather outfits down to the smallest spanner.

Don and Wilf had borrowed a van which was large enough to carry all three motorcycles and shared the driving on the long journey to the docks. Louie and Simmy travelled with Jack in his Jaguar and chatted non-stop all the way. The weather was kind to them and the journey went without a hitch. The voyage too was delightful, thanks to a calm sea and Louie and Simmy agreed that their first sight of the beautiful Isle of Man was unforgettable.

"What do you think of it?" Jack asked as he joined them on deck. They both grinned. "I knew you'd like it. After the race I'll have plenty of time to take you sight seeing."

The practice went well to be followed by the race the next day. Louie tried to convince herself that there was nothing to worry about. After all, Wilf had been racing in Germany and both he and Don had had plenty of experience racing in England, but when she saw them on the starting grid, a feeling of dread came over her. She watched with trepidation as they flashed by on the first circuit. After several more laps she began to relax thinking it must soon be over when it was announced over the loudspeaker that there had been an accident. She sensed that one of her boys had been hurt. She slipped away from the group of friends to try to get a close look as the stretcher was taken to the ambulance, Simmy was soon by her side.

"It's Don!" she cried running forward. Then someone was holding her back. "Please let me go. I'm his mother!" They were both helped into the ambulance and with sirens blaring they sped on their way to hospital. Don lay very still. Louie plucked up courage to ask the young ambulance man who was attending to him whether he was still alive?

He nodded, "He's concussed." He then carried on with his work to make him comfortable.

When they arrived at the hospital there was a flurry of activity. A nurse took Louie and Simmy to a small waiting room and gave them each a cup of tea.

"Is there any news?" asked Louie.

"The doctor will see you as soon as they know anything," and the nurse was gone, leaving Louie and Simmy to wait for what seemed an eternity.

At last the doctor came but his news did not exactly fill them with confidence. "He's taken quite a knock and is badly concussed. He's in a coma but is now stable and we'll know more in a day or two. I think it's best if you go back to your hotel and get some rest. We'll contact you if there's any change."

Jack arrived at the hospital anxious for news of Don. After the finish of the race he had heard about his crash as he returned his motorcycle to the pits. He hurriedly changed out of his leathers and drove to the hospital. As he drove Louie and Simmy back to their hotel he was able to reassure them that Wilf was safe.

"I couldn't find Wilf in the pits and was in such a hurry to get to the hospital I thought I'd try and find him later. Someone told me he finished fourth, which is a tremendous achievement for his first attempt in the Manx TT. I was only ninth but at least I finished the race this time."

Jack left Louie and Simmy at the hotel and returned to the race track to find Wilf who was having a drink with his friends unaware of what had happened to Don. He was very upset on hearing the news and immediately went with Jack to try to find Don's motorcycle. It was in a sorry state and they knew it was going to take a lot of rebuilding, they just hoped he would be well enough to ride it again.

Back at the hotel they waited for news but none came and when they telephoned the hospital it was always the same negative reply, "He's holding his own, but still in a coma."

The next day, after a sleepless night, they went to the hospital. Wilf and Louie were allowed to see Don while Jack and Simmy waited in the car. He was in a side ward and a nurse was by his bedside. Louie took his hand and held it firmly, willing him to live but he did not move. They returned the following day and still no sign of recovery.

"I think I'd like to walk back," said Louie.

"I'll come with you," said Simmy. "The walk will do us good." They made their way to the sea front while

Jack and Wilf drove back to the hotel. They walked along the sands among the scattering of holiday makers and came to a fairground with some amusement tents. Outside one of the smaller tents hung a sign: GYPSY LEE. FORTUNE TELLER. HALF A CROWN.

"Come on," said Simmy. "Let's see what she says." She thought it would take Louie's mind off her troubles for a short while. So, before she could refuse, Simmy pushed her into the tent. Gypsy Lee invited them to sit down, she was a middle-aged lady with a kindly weather-beaten face and appeared to be a genuine Romany. They placed their half crowns on her table.

Louie held back but the Gypsy took her hand and studied her palm then gazed into her crystal ball. After a while she said, "You're concerned about a member of your family who's very ill. Don't worry, my dear, he will recover."

Louie was taken aback and asked, "Why do you say 'he'?"

"You have sons and daughters but it's the condition of one of your sons that's causing you distress."

Next, she read Simmy's palm and somehow seemed to know that she was a widow and living with her daughter. She predicted that she would move away but had many happy years to look forward to.

As they were leaving her tent the Gypsy took hold of Louie's arm, "Your son will be fine. Try not to worry."

Louie and Simmy went on their way.

"What a load of old bunkum," said Louie. "I wish I could believe her."

The next day there was no improvement in Don's condition and she was feeling even more sceptical about Gypsy Lee's prophesy. The nurse suggested that she sit awhile and talk to him, the recognition of her voice could rouse him from his coma. She spent most of the afternoon chatting away about Wilf's success, the Isle of Man and their new home, Clanfield. She was not sure whether she could detect a slight movement in his eyelids but thought it was probably her imagination. However, she asked the nurse if she could return in the evening and the nurse readily agreed.

As she sat talking to him, slowly but surely his eyes opened. "Don. Oh Don!" Louie took his hand and gave it a squeeze. A passing nurse popped her head round the door to see what was happening and was soon by Louie's side giving her a little hug.

"He's got lovely brown eyes," she said, then she hurried off to tell the sister.

Just as Gypsy Lee had predicted Don was soon out of hospital and on the road to a full recovery, though Louie thought it would be wise to stay on for a few more days to get his strength back before the long journey home.

Meanwhile, Wilf had returned to Clanfield with the motorcycles and had already set about the task of repairing Don's machine. Doreen had assured Jack that Alfie was coping well at the garage and could manage without him so he was able to stay on as long as necessary.

Now that they were no longer so worried over Don's health Louie and Simmy were able to see a little more of the island. As they wandered around the town of

Douglas Louie spotted a Manx cat for sale in a pet shop. She thought it was a myth that they did not have a tail, but when she saw this tailless moggy she was so taken with it she made up her mind to take it home with her.

"I think I'll be the only person in Oxford to own a Manx cat," she said as she stroked its soft fur.

"I don't care that much for it," said Simmy. "It has a pretty enough face, I grant you, but I don't like the look of the other end."

"Then don't look at the other end," Louie laughed. She had to admit it did look a bit strange and wondered whether being bereft of its tail affected its balance when climbing. Also, how was she going to know when he was angry.

While Louie was away in the Isle of Man, George had taken a turn for the worse. He had been rushed into the Radcliffe Hospital for an emergency operation and was now back home again. Janet was very tired, she had been nursing him round the clock.

CHAPTER
TWELVE

Doreen received a letter from her landlord, Arthur Bellingham. He said he needed to sell the house and wondered if she would like to buy it? Most of the houses in that part of Oxford were leasehold. As a sitting tenant, Doreen was in a strong position to negotiate the price, but as there were only thirteen years left on the lease, she would have to consider his proposal very carefully. She talked it over with Jack.

"I don't know much about the value of property," he admitted. "I'll leave it up to you."

Doreen made an appointment to visit her solicitor, John Linnell, and walked the short distance to his office in Oxford. He was a kind man and a real friend and she valued his advice.

"I have the money my father left me," she said, "but with such a short lease I wouldn't want to pay too much for the house. I wondered whether to buy it and then sell it as a going concern. I don't want to spend the rest of my life running a guest house. Although I've met some very nice people, I've been at their beck and call seven days a week and there's little privacy. Jack's business is doing quite well now and he thinks we can manage financially. There are four flights of stairs in that house, sixty steps in all, I count them every day as I'm running up and down. My dream would be, eventually, to live in a bungalow. Meanwhile, anything smaller will do."

John Linnell looked thoughtful. "It's difficult to advise you as it may not be an easy house to sell, but if you're prepared to take a gamble, go ahead."

Doreen telephoned her mother that evening and told her what she planned to do. Louie agreed it would be a good idea, so she submitted a low offer. To her surprise it was accepted and she was now a property owner.

A month after the deal was completed she advertised the guest house for sale in the *Oxford Times* and the first couple to view fell in love with it and agreed to buy it providing they could move in as soon as possible.

Doreen started house hunting with a vengeance but with little success, she began to wonder if she was ever going to find anywhere suitable in time to bring off the deal.

Alfie wandered in one evening with the *Oxford Times* tucked under his arm. "There's a house for sale in Kidlington. It sounds quite nice, thought you might be interested," he said as he opened the paper to the page where he had marked the advertisement.

"They all sound nice until you see them," said Doreen. "This one seems to be a bargain, I'll telephone the owners straight away." She arranged to view it the following morning. After bundling Sylvia off to school, she managed to start her elderly little car and headed out of Oxford.

Kidlington was a popular village as it was situated only a few miles from the city centre. After looking around the house she decided it was the best she had seen so far. It was detached with large bay windows and a fair sized garden but, after living in Norham Road, the rooms seemed very small.

Doreen talked it over with Jack that evening and they decided to go ahead and buy the house. "It'll do to be going on with," she said. "We can always sell it and move on again if we don't like it."

In a short while they had moved to Kidlington. It was a lovely little house and Doreen should have been thrilled with it but somehow it didn't seem like home.

Doreen was driving up Cumnor Hill one day to visit her mother when she noticed a man standing at a bus stop. He looked like Henry Sloane, but she couldn't be sure as she only had a passing glimpse as she sped by in the car.

She found Louie working in the garden. "On the way here I thought I saw Henry Sloane waiting for a bus just down the road," she said. "I wondered if he'd been visiting you?"

"No. I haven't seen him for ages," Louie replied casually. "Anyway, he's got his own car. I shouldn't think he travels by bus."

"I was probably mistaken," said Doreen as she took up a spade and helped her mother with the digging. Manxy, the tailless cat, walked down the garden path to join them and purred affectionately when Louie downed tools to pick him up.

"Let's leave the gardening and make a cup of tea," she said. "I've got something to tell you." As they sat in the comfort of the spacious lounge, Louie showed Doreen the particulars of a house called Garfield which was situated near to the bottom of Cumnor Hill.

"Surely you're not thinking of moving already. This is such a lovely house. Aren't you happy here?" Doreen asked.

"Well Garfield has a hard tennis court and that nice young estate agent from James, Styles and Whitlock thought I might like it."

Doreen laughed, "Jack's going with Don and Wilf to race at Donnington Park tomorrow so I'll come over with Sylvia and we can look at it together."

It was a grand house set in a large garden with a path leading down to the tennis court. Louie stood gazing in admiration. "We could teach Sylvia to play." She loved tennis and was remembering the happy times she had had at the Thame Tennis Club before she was married.

Doreen could see that she was attracted to the house. "Do you think the boys will like it?" she asked as they trudged up the hill to Clanfield.

"I don't think either of them were listening when I told them about it," said Louie. "You know what they're like when they're preparing for a race. Their heads are full of motorbikes, motorbikes, motorbikes. They don't seem to mind where they live so I shall go ahead and make an offer for the house."

The charming young estate agent contacted Louie a week later to say that her offer had been accepted. She was thrilled and told him to put Clanfield on the market. In the meantime, she decided she needed a little help in the house, especially as she would be showing it to prospective buyers. An advertisement in the *Oxford*

Mail brought Mrs Hewer to her aid, housework was her forte, she seemed to really enjoy scouring and polishing. She was a gem.

Jack, Don and Wilf had had a successful trip to Donnington Park and though they did not win, all three were well placed. Don proved to have made a remarkable recovery after his accident and their motorcycles ran well. A group of their friends turned up to cheer them on and a good time was had by all.

A month went by and though Louie had shown several people around Clanfield no one had made so much as an offer. She started to worry that it might not sell. The estate agent suggested she sell Garfield instead as he thought he may have a buyer. One of their clients particularly wanted a house with a tennis court and she might even make a small profit. Louie reluctantly told him to go ahead. The client turned out to be a surgeon working at the Radcliffe Infirmary. Mr Gordon was a charming man and Louie became great friends with him and his lovely family, often joining them for a game of tennis. Mrs Hewer took on some cleaning for them too and while they were having their morning coffee, she kept Louie informed about all the "goings on" at Garfield.

"The doctor always insists that there's a pot of salad cream on the dinner table. He told me that one's body needs oil and that was a good way of ensuring the family were lubricated. Makes us sound like a lot of old engines," laughed Mrs Hewer. After this particular snippet of information, Louie made sure that salad cream was always available on her dining table and the boys said it went well with their chips.

Louie became more settled at Clanfield, she enjoyed gardening and grew plenty of vegetables for her own use as well as some to give away. She loved having the company of Don and Wilf and always looked forward to the visits from Jane and Olive and their boys. Life was pretty good until, early one morning, she had a telephone call from Janet to say that George had died in the night.

CHAPTER
THIRTEEN

Building was in progress on a new housing estate in Cowley, on the outskirts of Oxford, it was to be called Blackbird Leys. There was to be a corner shop for the sale of general provisions and Alfie's wife, Doris, had made a successful application to become the proprietor.

"I think it's going to be too much for her to manage on her own," Alfie told Jack. "I'll have to help her, so I'm afraid I won't be able to spend so much time at the garage but I'll do all I can."

"We'll manage somehow," Jack assured him, "even if we have to employ a young lad."

Jack could never resist an unusual motorcycle and although he had never even heard of the make, he bought a Japanese OEC, it had a 1000cc engine with duplex steering. It needed some restoration and he realized he was never going to find the time, so when Don took an interest in it, he sold it to him.

Don set about renovating the motorcycle and when he had completed its transformation, he rode it at every opportunity to show off his gleaming, powerful machine. Sadly, he was short of cash so decided to sell it, "needs must when the devil drives". Jack made an appointment for one of his friends to have a look at it.

Bert came from Banbury and liked to change his motorcycles frequently. He was always on the lookout for a bargain but had the reputation of being rather indecisive. Don gave the machine a final polish and waited. On his arrival, he proudly wheeled it out of the garage. Bert seemed truly smitten and took a long time to inspect every inch of it whilst repeatedly muttering to himself, "I don't know? Oh, I don't know?" Eventually, after much thought he plucked up courage to ask if he could have a ride on it. Don climbed onto the motorcycle and Bert perched behind him on the pillion, looking a little apprehensive. Don kicked up the machine, the powerful engine burst into life and Bert was nearly left behind as he opened the throttle and roared off down Cumnor Hill. Wilf stood transfixed as they disappeared into the distance. After a while they reappeared and Don pulled into the drive, his passenger looked decidedly pale as he clung on for dear life. Bert dismounted and walked a little unsteadily towards his car.

"It might be too powerful for me," he murmured, "but I'll think about it and let you know." The boys, however, were pretty sure that he had already come to the decision not to buy the motorcycle.

Janet had moved to a smaller house on the Iffley Road, her previous home held too many memories and she needed to get away. The new house was modern with a small garden and was easily maintained so, after the initial shock of George's death had worn off, she felt ready to start a new enterprise. There was a cottage for sale locally that sounded interesting so she telephoned

Doreen to see if she could go with her that afternoon to have a look at. It was situated in Iffley village, on the outskirts of Oxford, down a lane that led to the famous Iffley Lock. It was a popular area for sightseers and walkers where you could watch the lock-keeper at work going through the complicated ritual of helping the boats through the lock gates and on their way. It was a charming cottage with a large garden, though rather dilapidated. The previous owners had sold cold drinks and snacks. Doreen could tell that Janet had set her heart on it.

It was not long before she had moved in and was working hard to turn Tudor Cottage into her dream home. Her intention was to run a small exclusive restaurant. There was a pleasant beamed room suitable for the dining room but spoiled by a modern fireplace, so Janet plucked up courage and pulled it out to reveal an old bread oven which became an attractive feature and talking point for the diners. The garden, now free of weeds, supplied fresh vegetables for the kitchen. Tudor Cottage with its charming Old World atmosphere coupled with Janet's culinary expertise soon became a popular eating place and she had little time left to grieve.

Doreen was not entirely happy with her home in Kidlington, it was an awkward distance from Jack's work and Sylvia's school. Despite her efforts, the garden was disappointing due to the clay soil and leaky septic tank. She saw an advertisement for a bungalow that seemed so reasonably priced she decided to view it at the first opportunity. She drove to Bickerton Road in

Headington to have a little peep at the outside before bothering the agents for the key. She spotted the property behind a high hedge and could see straight away why it was so cheap. It was constructed of wood. However, it was very attractive and stood on an exceptionally large plot in a pleasant road. Doreen headed for the agent's office to ask for the key and then to Cumnor Hill to see if her mother would go with her to look inside. Louie loved looking at property and was soon in the car. There was a veranda round the front door and when they went inside they were surprised at the size of the rooms. They wandered round the large overgrown garden and came across an orchard with numerous apple trees.

"What do you think?" asked Doreen.

Louie thought for a while, "I love it. If I were you, I'd be very tempted to buy it."

That evening Jack and Sylvia were given a guided tour of the bungalow and Doreen waited with baited breath for their verdict, she had already decided that she wanted to live in this unusual but charming property. Sylvia was happily exploring the garden, there was no need to ask if she would be happy to live there and it was evident that Jack liked it too.

The agents told Doreen that there had been plenty of interest in the property but it was not possible to get a mortgage on a wooden bungalow and the insurance would be very high, so, no one had as yet made an offer. She could hardly wait to contact the agents the following morning and soon her offer of £1,500 was accepted.

She hoped she had done the right thing, but there was no going back now. She found a large sheet of cardboard, painted a sign: HOUSE FOR SALE, and displayed it in her front window. Luckily, that very evening, an elderly couple came to the door asking to view the house. Doreen showed them round and, to her amazement, after a quick inspection they said they would like to buy it.

After that, all went smoothly and they were soon settled in their new home. It needed considerable refurbishment but the new electric wiring had been completed and the gas man had installed the cooker, making sure to show Doreen where to turn off the gas at the mains in case of emergency, though, with so much to do, his instructions went in one ear and out of the other. She finished painting the bathroom and when the paint was dry, gave the all clear to Jack, who was to be the first to christen the new bath. As he was getting dressed he thought he could detect a smell of burning paint, then he heard a roaring noise coming from the loft and a brown patch appeared on the ceiling. They were mystified as to what was happening.

"Don's an electrician," said Jack. "He'll know what to do, I'll go and get him."

"Do hurry!" Doreen called out as she watched him run to the car. It was then she realized that she had forgotten to contact the insurance company to cover her new home and cancel the old policy. Now in a panic, she rushed to the kitchen, grabbed a table and placed it under the entrance to the loft. She clambered onto the table and lifted the wooden cover to reveal fires flaring in three different places. She scrambled down and grabbed some cushions from the lounge and a kitchen chair which she placed on top of the table. Cursing the fact that she had never got round to buying a ladder, she hauled herself through the aperture and tried to quench the flames with a cushion, but as soon as she took the cushion away something seemed to ignite the fire again. By now, she had burnt her hands and scorched her hair and eyebrows and, as she stood transfixed looking at the scene, she realized that the flames were coming from the gas pipes. She quickly made her way back to the opening but, when she looked down she discovered that the chair had toppled off the table and she could not see how she was going to get down. There was no one to call to and she was very frightened. She managed to lie on her stomach and dangle her legs towards the table, dropping onto it with a thud. Trying to remember what the gas man had told her, she searched the kitchen and found the tap in a cupboard. She turned it off and listened, the roaring noise had stopped!

Don and Jack came running into the hall, stopped short when they saw the state Doreen was in and helped her onto the settee. "I think the fire's out," she gasped, "but the rafters are still smouldering." After they made sure everything was safe, Don explained that there had been an electrical short which had ignited the rather old gas pipes.

"I really thought we'd lost our home," Doreen said later. After a wash and change of clothes she was feeling better but her hands and face were sore and she had lost her eyebrows. Then, instead of congratulating her on her heroism, Jack and Don scolded her for being so reckless.

142

* * *

There was a small private school within walking distance from Bickerton Road so it made sense for Sylvia to enrol there and save the journey to Banbury Road each day. At the end of term she left Greycotes School and continued her education with Miss Welch at her small establishment in Beech Road where she soon made friends and settled down.

Doreen had become friendly with a lady called Lil Chandler who lived opposite them. She had recently lost her husband and had taken a job in a business agency in Oxford and was to become a lifelong friend of all the family.

CHAPTER
FOURTEEN

Janet had bought a caravan and her great joy was to spend a few nights away and take her corgi dog, Bonny, which she adored, for long walks. It was difficult to leave the restaurant for too long, so she frequently visited the New Forest as she could drive there in under two hours. Often, friends would accompany her and a girl called Isabel, who worked in the restaurant, took to the caravan trips like a duck to water. Janet was convinced that both she and Isabel must have been Gypsies in a previous life.

Having become skilful in towing the caravan behind her large car, Janet decided it was time to be more adventurous and planned a trip to the continent. She invited Isabel and Edith to go with her. Whilst driving in Amsterdam, they were so intrigued with their surroundings that the morning had flown by and they had left it late to find somewhere to have lunch. They parked the car and caravan in a quiet suburb and set off on foot in search of a restaurant. They walked a considerable distance through a residential area and still no sign of an eating place. By now they were ravenous and very tired so decided to catch a bus. After a long wait one appeared and they thankfully clambered aboard. They didn't know which way the bus was heading and it seemed to be travelling in circles but luckily the conductor spoke English and assured them they would soon be in the town centre and directed them to a good restaurant. Their stomachs were rattling with hunger and Edith and Isabel were hard on Janet's heels as she led the way. It was an excellent meal and they left the establishment very much refreshed. As they stood on the pavement outside they realized they didn't know which way to go and could not remember the name of the street where the car and caravan were parked. They took a vote as to whether they go left or right. Right it was, so they started walking and walking, eventually reaching the outskirts of Amsterdam, but no sign of their vehicle. It was getting dark and it felt eerie in the dimly lit deserted streets.

"I can't go much farther," said Edith. "I think I've got a blister."

"Well we can't stop here, you'll have to force yourself," Janet urged, taking her arm. They trundled on and just as they felt they could not walk another step, they turned a corner and there, before them, stood the car and caravan.

Mrs Prior's husband, also named George, had died and sadly their farm had been sold and she now lived in a bungalow in Carterton. She missed George more than she could say and she also missed the farm and all her good friends and neighbours in Filkins. Janet suggested to Louie that they invite her to go with them for a holiday in the caravan, it would be a new experience for her and she readily accepted their invitation.

The weather was perfect the following weekend so Janet loaded the car with goodies and together with Bonny they set off for the New Forest. They found an idyllic spot to park and indulged in a sumptuous lunch before taking Bonny for a walk. Janet then unhitched the caravan and drove back to Tudor Cottage leaving the two ladies for a week to enjoy the beauty of the Forest. Though great friends, they never called each other by their Christian names, Mrs Prior was always Mrs Prior and Louie was always Mrs Hutt. They quarrelled constantly and enjoyed every minute.

Jack had bought a television set. No one else owned one in the area and when the aerial appeared on their chimney in Bickerton Road it caused quite a stir. It was like peering through a snowstorm and the black and white picture frequently turned somersaults, but to see Mary Malcolm reading the news was quite something.

Sylvia's favourite programme was Muffin the Mule. Muffin was a string puppet and danced on a piano accompanied by Annette Mills, the sister of the famous actor John Mills. Jack had bought Sylvia a new bicycle for her birthday and after a ride out with her best friend, Graham, who lived a few doors away, it was back home for a birthday tea and Children's Hour on television.

Doreen invited Lil and her elderly mother to tea and afterwards proudly switched on the television. She couldn't help smiling when she saw the look on the old lady's face as she watched the pictures form on the screen. The reception was good that evening and she was so enjoying herself that when it was time to go, Lil had difficulty in persuading her mother to leave. She would never forget her introduction to this new craze called television.

Lil was a great reader and had always got her nose in a book but she was fascinated with this latest home entertainment and on the slightest pretext she frequently popped in at viewing time hoping the set was turned on.

On one of her visits Lil told Doreen and Jack of the latest scandal in Bickerton Road. When he came home from the garage Jack would use any car that was handy, so different cars were left parked outside the bungalow. This intrigued the neighbours who came to the conclusion that Doreen was a "bad lot". This amused Jack and he pulled her leg unmercifully until she decided to retaliate and asked him how it felt to be a dirty old man visiting a house of ill repute.

Janet's cuisine had become so popular that she was having difficulty accommodating all her clientele in the confined space of Tudor Cottage. She loved it there but thought the only answer would be to find somewhere larger to run her restaurant. Lil contacted her from work to say that a property had just come on their books that might suit her.

It was a large house in the centre of Woodstock and had once been the local grammar school. It was rather dilapidated but solidly built of Cotswold stone and the rooms were of such ample proportions that Janet felt she could really spread her wings. The house was so large that she would also have room to take in paying guests. It was a challenge she could not refuse so she bought it and, after months of hard work, transformed it into a worthy successor to Tudor Cottage. It was rumoured that Elizabeth I had visited Woodstock and that her staff had stayed at an inn called The Pied Bull, but as no such inn now existed, Janet thought it would be a fitting name for her new establishment.

It was a very warm day and Louie had been shopping at her local grocery store which was about a mile from home. She started the long walk up the hill lugging her baskets, wishing she had not been tempted to buy so much. When running the guest house she had been used to buying provisions in large quantities and now tended to over estimate the amount she needed.

A car pulled up just in front of her and the driver jumped out. "Oh, it's you, Henry!" She gasped in surprise.

"It looks as if you need a helping hand," he said. "Come on, let me give you a lift." He took hold of her baskets and stowed them in the boot of his car. She had to admit that her legs were aching and gratefully climbed into the passenger seat. He parked near to her front door and carried her shopping into the house.

"It's such a hot day. Would you like a drink?" asked Louie.

"A cup of tea would be lovely," he answered, "but I don't want to put you to any trouble."

They sat in a cool spot under a tree in the garden. They found so much to talk about that the afternoon soon passed.

"You have a lovely home, Louie," said Henry.

"I quite like living here. However, from what you tell me, your home is far more impressive."

"It is an impressive house but it's not a home," he said. "There's no comfort. Every piece of furniture Mildred buys has to be grander and more expensive than anyone else's. It's designed more to show off than to live in. Not what I would choose. Still, as long as it keeps her happy."

"Is she happy?" asked Louie.

"Oh yes. Her days seem to revolve around dressing up for dinner parties and playing bridge. She's in her element. I'm the one who's unhappy. Sometimes I wish I'd never met her."

Just then the garden gate opened with a rattle and Doreen and Sylvia appeared.

"There you are," said Doreen. "We've been looking for you, I might have known you'd be in the garden. Hello, Henry. Isn't it a lovely day?"

"Yes, the weather's grand," he said, standing up and searching in his pockets for his car keys. "I'd better be getting back. Mildred will be wondering where I am."

They walked with him to his car and waved him goodbye as the large car swept down the drive and disappeared through the gateway. Louie suddenly remembered that she had invited Doreen and Sylvia for tea.

"Go and sit in the garden," she said. "I'll soon have tea ready." She hurried into the kitchen to put the kettle on.

"We didn't mean to intrude," said Doreen later as they sat round the garden table eating scones with home-made plum jam. "I didn't know that Henry would be here."

"You weren't intruding," laughed Louie. "You make it sound as if we were having a clandestine meeting. He was only giving me a lift with my shopping. By the way, have you seen Wilf this week?"

"No, not for while," Doreen replied. "Is he all right?"

"Well, don't let him know I've told you, but he's met a charming girl called Rosemary, she's so pretty. She's a nursing sister and works at a private maternity home. I know you'll like her."

After tea they picked peas from the vegetable garden, then sat on the veranda podding them as they talked.

Later that evening, when Doreen and Jack had time to themselves to sit and talk, Doreen told him about the enjoyable afternoon they had spent with her mother. "We found her sitting in the garden with Henry Sloane. He soon left when we arrived. You don't think there's anything going on, do you?"

Jack laughed, "Of course not. Henry would be too frightened of Mildred to go astray."

Doreen did not pursue the matter but still felt that her mother was hiding something. "Well, what sort of a day have you had?" she asked, changing the subject.

"I had a visit from a dissatisfied customer," said Jack. "Alfie had sold him a car nearly two years ago and he came storming in complaining that it was not running as it should. He was in quite a temper and stood kicking one of the front tyres that was worn, he expected me to replace it. I looked under the bonnet and there was not a spot of oil on the dipstick nor water in the radiator. I asked him when it had last been checked and he said his daughter had been using the car. How was she supposed

150

to know about things like that? I filled it up with oil and water and then it transpired that he'd only paid twenty five pounds for it and he still thought I was going to replace the tyre, so I sent him on his way."

"What did you say to him?" Doreen was laughing fit to bust.

"Nothing that I could repeat in front of a lady," he chuckled.

When Doreen and Sylvia next visited Louie, they met Rosemary when Wilf brought her home to tea. They really liked her and Doreen could tell that her brother was very much in love.

Rosemary was born and brought up in the Welsh border county of Radnorshire and was the fifth of six girls. Her father, John, was a farmer's son. After serving abroad in the army throughout the war, he decided not to return to farming and joined the Police Force. Sadly, Rosemary's mother, Jinny, died of pneumonia when she was only three years old. Consequently, the girls spent most of their childhood days on their grandparents' farm. Although times were hard they were always well fed and made to feel welcome. At the age of fifteen, she travelled to Birmingham to begin her nursing training. Now a qualified nursing sister, she had come to Oxford with a friend as it was a convenient place to live and work while they made arrangements to emigrate to Australia, a country that was crying out for trained nurses.

Later, when Rosemary and Wilf had gone for a walk, Louie told Doreen in confidence that she hoped

151

Rosemary would not be going to Australia. She felt sure that she was the girl that Wilf was going to marry, they seemed so happy together.

On reaching home Doreen was surprised that Jack had not returned. She prepared supper, but still no sign of him. Maybe he was still at the garage. He had bought a Rolls-Royce Silver Cloud and had been spending some time restoring it, but when she telephoned there was no reply. When at last she heard his car and Sylvia ran out to meet him, he was lifting a large cardboard box from the back seat. Together they went indoors and he put the box down on the kitchen floor.

"You open it, Sylvia," he said. She cautiously opened the lid and then gasped with joy as she lifted out an adorable black and white cocker spaniel puppy. "I delivered a car to a customer and he talked me into buying it."

Doreen guessed he had not taken much persuading as she stroked its soft silky coat. "He's the image of Rover," she said. Rover was one of the dogs that was kept on the farm where she lived as a girl. "What shall we call him?"

"Spot," Sylvia pointed to the speckles on his nose. So Spot he was.

CHAPTER
FIFTEEN

While chatting to her mother on the telephone, Doreen sensed that something was afoot and decided to pay a visit to Clanfield. Sylvia was eager to go too as she was longing to show her granny the puppy. Louie was pleased to see them and they were joined by Mrs Hewer for a cup of coffee.

After Mrs Hewer had returned to her chores and much had been made of the puppy, Louie told Doreen that she had had a visit from John Brooks, the estate agent.

"I know what you're going to say," Doreen laughed. "He's taken you to see a house."

"Well yes, it's on the Woodstock Road. It seems such a bargain but it needs some renovation. Shall we go and have a look at it? It's empty but I've got the keys."

They soon arrived outside a very large house with an exceedingly overgrown garden and Doreen had difficulty in opening the drive gates as the hinges had rusted away. She managed to drag them open and parked the car close to the front door, which was sadly in need of a coat of paint as was the whole house.

"What do you think?" asked Louie after they had walked from room to neglected room.

"It mostly needs a lick of paint and a good tidy up in the garden. Have you told Mr Rose?" Doreen was quite enthusiastic.

"Mr Rose is coming on Monday, but I'm glad you've seen it first. If he likes it shall I have a go?"

"You really are incorrigible," said Doreen, giving her mother a hug. "Why ask me? You know you'll make up your own mind anyway. I think it has great potential."

On the Monday evening Louie telephoned to say that Mr Rose was in agreement and she was going to buy the Woodstock Road house. "Mr Rose thinks his daughter might buy Clanfield, he told me that she's always liked it."

So the move went ahead and Louie, Don and Wilf were soon living in the somewhat dilapidated house surrounded with paint pots, stepladders, dust sheets and plumbing equipment. It was springtime and the weather was fine so the work was soon completed. The house was restored to its former glory and Louie was very pleased with her purchase.

Months of hard work and upheaval had left Louie feeling tired and in need of a break, so she telephoned Mrs Prior and Simmy telling them that she intended to take a holiday and inviting them to join her. "I rather fancy Ireland," she said and they both agreed they would love to go as, like Louie, they had never been there. She went ahead and booked for them all to go for a fortnight on a coach tour.

Doreen took them to the bus station at Gloucester Green in Oxford and they were soon aboard a very smart coach waving goodbye. As she drove home she thought about Don and Wilf fending for themselves but as they both had girlfriends she guessed they would be fine. Don had met a lovely girl called Evelyn, her surname was West though no relation to Jack. She felt sure that both her brothers had met their life partners and, should that be the case, how lucky she would be to gain two more sisters. She stopped to do some shopping, then hurried home when she remembered that she had left the puppy far too long and he might have made a mess in the kitchen. He was nearly house-trained though could not be expected to wait on his own for too long, but all was well, so she gave him a hug and took him for a walk.

The holiday in Ireland was going well, the weather was perfect and Louie, Mrs Prior and Simmy were enjoying the Irish fare. It was a case of "when in Rome" as they had become quite addicted to a glass of Guinness with their evening meal.

However, "two's company, three's a crowd" and the three ladies found it difficult to agree. Often, Louie found herself acting as mediator. Simmy wanted to have a ride on a jogging cart but Mrs Prior didn't.

"I've ridden in better carts than that," she said.

"So have I," said Louie. "But this is part of the fun of coming to Ireland and we're not going to disappoint Simmy, are we?"

Mrs Prior grudgingly relented and they climbed aboard and took their seats. The horse was urged into a trot and they were soon enjoying views of the delightful countryside. Louie was reminded of her farming days when she had her own pony and trap. She would like to

155

have taken the reins and driven the lovely old horse herself, even though it did not compare with her high stepping Polly. She was aroused from her nostalgia when, as they passed a crofter's cottage, a collie dog came running into the road to snap and bark at the heels of the horse, frightening it into a frenzied gallop. The three friends clung to the cart and to each other. "I told you I didn't want to come," complained Mrs Prior, but she was soon laughing with the others when the driver finally regained control of the horse. The dog, having caused enough excitement for one day, turned tail and ran back to the cottage.

Everywhere they went there were donkeys of various sizes and colours, some carrying quite large loads and others pulling carts. They seemed to be very strong for such small animals and all had the same self-important way of toddling along. Louie would have loved to take one home for Sylvia but that would not have been very practical so she took plenty of photographs instead.

The days flew by and it was time to go home. When Doreen met them at the bus station she had changed her car. Her previous one was an Austin tourer, it was good and reliable but was painted in an army style camouflage paint and she never liked it. So, when Jack came home one day in a green, four seater, Singer sports car, she persuaded him to swap it. It was a sunny day and the hood was down so the ladies climbed in and tied on their head scarves.

"This is great," said Simmy as they sped off through the centre of Oxford.

Having taken Simmy and Mrs Prior home, Doreen drove Louie to Woodstock Road and they started to unload her suitcases.

"I've just remembered, there's something I had to tell you," said Doreen. "I read in the *Oxford Times* last week that Mildred's dead."

Louie was shocked. "What do you mean dead? She can't be dead!"

"Apparently, she was knocked down by a bus in the High Street. The funeral was last Monday."

"Oh dear. I shall have to write to Henry and send my condolences," said Louie. "I shan't know what to say. Poor Mildred and poor Henry."

Later that evening she sat down to write to him. After their last meeting, when he had told her of his unhappy life with Mildred, she found it a very difficult letter to write. She even wondered whether to telephone him but when she dialled his number there was no reply. Whatever his feelings for her recently he must have loved her at some time and he must be devastated now. At last, she finished the letter and walked to the post box with a heavy heart. After her jolly holiday Louie felt stunned by Mildred's death.

The weather forecast was good so Doreen telephoned Edith to see if she and Jacky would like to come and stay for a few days. As Jacky was not able to get away, it was decided that Doreen, Sylvia and Joan would drive to Weston-super-Mare to collect Edith. They arranged to make an early start so that they could spend some time by the sea.

Six o'clock the next morning Doreen was knocking on Joan's door. They set off in the little sports car and reached Weston in good time after an enjoyable journey. There had been hardly any traffic on the road at that time of day and they were soon being welcomed by their friends in Jubilee Road.

Jacky was a well known character in the area and in his spare time he kept a smallholding where he reared pigs and chickens. This was situated about half a mile from his home so he had bought a bicycle with a large carrier on the front which had previously been used for grocery deliveries and pedalled back and forth wearing his deerstalker hat. His Scottie dog, proudly wearing his little tartan jacket, rode in the carrier, a sight once seen never forgotten. After a guided tour round the smallholding, where Jacky collected fresh eggs for his visitors to take home, he then took them to see the donkeys that gave rides on the sands. When they were not working they were turned out to graze in a field which was used by the council as a refuse tip. They liked to scavenge in the rubbish and as a consequence the young ones sometimes got their hooves caught in discarded tins. Jacky liked to keep an eye on them and give a hand when they were in trouble.

They had so enjoyed their day at the seaside and were well on their way home when Doreen saw steam coming from under the bonnet and the engine smelt rather hot. Conveniently, there was a public house about a hundred yards up the road so she drove onto the forecourt. There were quite a few people sitting outside enjoying their drinks in the evening sunshine. All heads turned in her direction as Doreen lifted the bonnet, unscrewed the radiator cap and jumped out of the way as a jet of steam shot into the air.

"I'll go and get some drinks," she said, "then I can ask for some water."

She came back triumphantly with a tray of drinks in one hand and a jug of water in the other.

"I wouldn't pour it in yet," a young man ventured. "Let her cool down a bit." So they enjoyed their drinks and "let her cool". After a while, Doreen caught the young man's eye. "Should be all right now," he nodded.

She poured the water into the radiator but realized it was going to take more than this small jugful to fill it.

"We'll have to have another drink," she said and took the tray back to order the same again.

She emptied the jug. "It's not full yet. Drink up." Back she went again and still not full. By this time the barman had become curious and looked out of the window to see what was happening to the jugs of water. When Doreen next returned to the bar she found a large watering can full of water waiting for her.

"You don't have to buy drinks just to get some water," the barman smiled. Thanking him, she took the can. "Have you far to go?" he asked as he bent down behind the bar and emerged with two large empty cider bottles. "I'll fill these with water for you to take with you. You must have an almighty leak."

"Can I ask one more favour?" she said, by now she was quite embarrassed. "We all need to use the loo."

"I'm not surprised," he laughed and pointed to the toilet door.

With the radiator filled to the brim and the gin and tonics boosting her confidence, Doreen pressed the self-starter. The engine sprang to life and all seemed well. As they drove away the spectators cheered and waved them on their way. They stopped a couple of times to top up the radiator from the cider bottles and thankfully the little car reached home safely. Jack soon mended the leak the next day.

They spent an enjoyable week touring around in the open sports car to see places of interest and visit friends. When it was time for Edith to leave Jack decided to take her home in the Rolls-Royce. He had been working on the engine and thought a trip to Weston would be a good road test. Wearing his chauffeur's cap and a cheeky grin, he held the door open while Edith and Doreen majestically took their places on the rear seat, where they rode in style to Jubilee Road.

Spot was a grand little dog, he was very affectionate but, although he was not fully grown, he would guard the house and bark at strangers. Doreen enjoyed taking him for walks and would often take him to a delightful stretch of common land set on a hill nearby, called Shotover, where he could run free along the grassy tracks between the gorse bushes and bracken. Then, when he began to tire, it was a gentle walk down the hill back to Bickerton Road. She had just returned home one day and was preparing dinner, when the telephone rang.

"I'm Sister White speaking from the Blood Donor Department at The Churchill Hospital. Can you come round straight away Mrs West?"

160

"Of course," Doreen sensed the urgency in the Sister's voice. She had been a regular blood donor, so when she moved to Bickerton Road, which was very close to the hospital, she agreed to be on call when they needed blood for an emergency. She switched off the cooker and took off her apron as she ran to the car.

The sister was waiting for her and after she had given the precious blood it was time for tea and biscuits and she learnt that they were trying to save the life of a very poorly baby boy.

A fortnight later a letter arrived to say that the baby had survived and was doing well and would she like to come to see him? Not being able to resist the invitation, she visited the hospital that afternoon and was allowed to cuddle the frail little chap.

Doreen attended a meeting for parents at Sylvia's school and after the usual progress reports, Miss Welch, the headmistress told the assembly that she would be retiring at the end of term and the school would be closing down. Doreen's heart sank. It was going to be difficult to find such an excellent school and like the other parents she dreaded the upheaval. Sylvia had been happy there and was enjoying her work. Finally, it was decided that she would attend Sunnymede House School on the Banbury Road in Oxford.

Sylvia was keen to tell her parents about her first day at her new school. She liked the headmistress, Miss Webster, and her favourite lesson of the day was Art taught by Miss Bradwell.

Doreen was intrigued, "I used to be taught by a Miss Bradwell when I was at Burford Grammar School. We all loved her and called her 'Braddy'. I wonder if it could be the same lady?" She telephoned the school the next morning and was amazed to discover that it was indeed the same Miss Bradwell. Doreen's invitation to tea was readily accepted and Braddy soon became a regular visitor.

She had always been patient with her pupils and Doreen could only remember one occasion when she raised her voice. The schoolroom faced the playground and beyond was a clear view of Burford Church. This particular morning Doreen's concentration had wandered from her lesson and as she gazed out of the window she was remembering the embarrassing time when she attended the church with the other school boarders and had been terribly sick before she could leave her place in the pew. She had felt so ashamed. Her reminiscing was interrupted when, to her astonishment, she saw a man climbing up the side of the steeple. She was completely mesmerized and all thoughts of the lesson had disappeared. "Doreen!" Miss Bradwell's usually gentle voice, now so brusque, brought her back to earth but she still could not take her eyes from the window. Miss Bradwell walked to her desk and followed her gaze, the other children were craning their necks and little gasps were heard as they clapped eyes on the figure now nearing the top of the spire. They gathered round their teacher to watch while she told them about steeplejacks and their work. They all agreed it was not a career they would have wanted to pursue.

* * *

It was about a month after Louie had written to Henry and she had not heard from him. He had been in her thoughts lately and she wondered if he was all right. Then, one morning, a letter came from him postmarked Singapore. He thanked her for her condolences and told her that he had had to get away for a while and was staying with friends. He was selling most of his furniture and had put his house on the market. When he returned to England he would probably buy a flat. He hoped that Louie would keep in touch as he greatly valued her friendship.

She decided that she would write to him now and then. *I can keep him up to date with the local news, she thought. Let him know he still has friends here who are thinking of him.*

CHAPTER
SIXTEEN

The renovations on Louie's Woodstock Road house were now complete and she thought she ought to take a few paying guests. She had no state pension as Algy had never contributed for any insurance stamps because, at that time, it was not compulsory for people who were self-employed. Although she was over sixty years old she had no regular income and had to rely on her own money-making schemes which included taking in paying guests and moving house if the opportunity arose to make a profit. Luckily, she was fit and healthy for her age.

When Edwin was in the navy a portion of his pay had been taken to provide insurance so that if anything happened to him his mother would have a small pension. After his death some officials came to her house to assess her lifestyle and decided that, as she had a comfortable home and an income from her paying guests, she did not need it. It seemed sad that she never received a penny from the pension that Edwin had trustingly paid for. Louie contacted her local member of parliament, Quintin Hogg, who later became Lord Hailsham and told him what had happened. He was very concerned and brought the matter up in parliament but to no avail. Doreen often wondered what had happened to the money they took from her brother's meagre pay and felt it was a poor reward for dying in defence of his country.

Louie's first and only paying guest in her new home was a bank manager and seemed very pleasant, but when she discovered him playing golf in his bedroom on her precious Indian carpet, she asked him very diplomatically to find other accommodation.

"There's a time and a place for everything," she told Doreen. "Golf courses are the place to play golf. I'd have let him practice in the garden if he'd asked."

Doreen laughed. "You know you wouldn't have wanted him to turn your lawn into a putting green."

"Well, I'm relieved he's gone. What am I going to do now? This house is far too large for me. When the boys are not here, I feel like a pea in a drum rattling around here on my own. There's a house for sale on the Banbury Road, would you take me to see it? I can get the keys in the morning."

They viewed the house the next day, it was not too big and quite modern and they both thought it would suit Louie. So, after a telephone call to Mr Rose, arrangements were made to buy the Banbury Road house and put the other one on the market and Louie was on the move again.

Lil was a keen motorist and had passed her advanced driving test. She had been awarded a badge as a reward for her skills and this was proudly displayed together with her AA badge on the front of her smart black

Morris Minor car. There was nothing she enjoyed more than a drive to see her friend Janet in Woodstock, followed by a nice meal in the restaurant before taking a scenic route home.

On one of her visits Janet mentioned that she had been feeling very tired of late. Running a restaurant was one thing but running a restaurant and a guest house was too much for a girl on her own. She had excellent staff, but it was a big responsibility and she had even wondered whether to sell the business just to have a little time to herself.

"It sounds as if you need a complete rest," said Lil. "So there's no point in telling you about a property that's just come on our books."

"You'll have to tell me now," laughed Janet, "otherwise I shan't sleep tonight for curiosity."

"It's a very old building in the centre of Abingdon, built of wattle and daub with lots of old beams. Lately it's been run as a tearoom."

Janet was fascinated, "I suppose there's no harm in having a look. How soon can you make an appointment for me to view?"

She was shown around The Gargoyle Tea Rooms the following afternoon and in spite of the dingy atmosphere she knew she had to buy it. She needed a fresh challenge. Even before she reached home she had decided on a new name: The Pied Piper Restaurant.

Lil put the wheels in motion and soon found a buyer for The Pied Bull. Janet set about her new project with a vengeance. Her family worried that, as usual, she was working too hard.

166

Doreen was missing the independence she had when running the guest house and preferred to make her own contribution to the family income. When Joan mentioned that the hairdressing business that she used to run had come up for sale, she wondered if this was the opportunity she had been looking for.

"If I bought the business, do you think I could learn hairdressing?" she asked Joan.

Joan was cautious. "You could, but it would take quite a while and in the meantime the business would not be earning any money. If you employed a qualified hairdresser to run it for you while you learn the ropes you might be able to manage. I'll help in any way I can and I'll take you to London and introduce you to the wholesalers I used to deal with."

Jack agreed to go with Doreen to view the property although he was sceptical about her becoming a hairdresser.

When they arrived at 22, Eden Drive, Headington, on the outskirts of Oxford, they were both very impressed. The house comprised of comfortable living accommodation, a spacious well-fitted salon and a pleasant garden.

Doreen had some sleepless nights wondering what to do but since the fire in Bickerton Road she had never been entirely happy there and decided not to miss this chance to start a new career. Bungalows were few and far between, so when she put it on the market she was surprised how many people came to view. The stumbling block, however, was its wooden construction and no one made an offer. Eventually, a rich gentleman from London offered a good price, having been attracted by its unusual appearance and total privacy. He was looking for a "love nest" to spend naughty weekends with his mistress and it just fitted the bill.

On the day they were to move Doreen, Jack and Sylvia were all suffering from a dreadful bout of influenza and had had to return to their beds. Doreen telephoned the removal firm to put them off for a few days but they said they were fully booked for the next month, so they would have to move them beds and all! Luckily, Doreen had a good friend who came to their aid. Edna, who lived near Eden Drive, opened up the new home, lit the boiler, made tea and soon had the removal men working like clockwork. She didn't leave until the family were fed and warmly tucked up in bed. Doreen would never forget her kindness.

On a later visit, Edna told Doreen that her niece, Margaret, was a hairdresser and worked for an Oxford salon. She was married and lived quite near in Headington.

"I wonder if she'd come to work for me?" asked Doreen. "I'd love to meet her."

A meeting was arranged and they took to each other straight away. Margaret was an attractive girl, full of fun, and she agreed to run the salon until Doreen qualified, then she would leave to start a family.

It was unfortunate that the opening of the salon under Doreen's ownership coincided with a new invention that became all the rage, the home perm. The hairdressing trade was hit badly, making it an uphill struggle at first, but as satisfied customers spread the news of Margaret's skills the trade picked up. Doreen worked as an apprentice under her supervision, sweeping up hair, washing towels, cleaning mirrors, making appointments and acting as general dogsbody. She enjoyed the work, especially chatting to the customers and looked forward to the time when Margaret felt she could trust her with the scissors!!

Every two or three weeks she drove to London with Joan to visit the wholesalers. Afterwards, they enjoyed shopping and browsing in the Oxford Street stores. Doreen mostly browsed having already spent her money on necessities for the salon.

She had been promoted to shampooing the customers' hair and was feeling quite confident, so, when Margaret told her that a friend of hers was willing to let her practice her perming skills, she was delighted but a little apprehensive. Winding the hair round the small perming rollers looked so easy when Margaret did it, but when she attempted it she could not believe how difficult it was, the wretched hair went everywhere except round the rollers. She wondered if she would ever get the hang of it. She toiled away all morning and by lunch time she still hadn't finished. She gave her customer some lunch and carried on. After tea and cakes, late in the afternoon, her patient client emerged from the salon looking like a film star. Doreen had apologized for taking so long, but she said she'd be glad to let her practice again, apart from the free perm she'd had a most entertaining day.

* * *

A friend of Jack's had four acres of land for sale and offered it to him at a very reasonable price. It had been part of a disused airfield and there was a wide concrete drive running through the middle. It was in a secluded spot in the country about four miles from Oxford. After talking it over with Doreen he decided to buy it and give up his garage in Denmark Street. It was a big step to take and there would be a great deal of work to do, but to set up his business on his own land and not have to pay rent was very tempting. The first priority was to establish a water supply, which meant laying a considerable length of plastic piping to connect to the mains.

By the time Louie heard about the pipe laying operation the work had been completed. "I could probably have saved you the trouble," she said. "Didn't Doreen tell you I can divine water?" Louie discovered she had the gift of finding water when she lived on her father's farm. She held a divining rod, which was a V shaped hazel stick, in both hands and walked to and fro across the fields until the stick jerked violently and pointed to the ground. Her father had complete faith in her talent and excavated two wells at sites she had indicated, these had been very successful and never ran dry. When she was a young girl, her party piece was to find a gold sovereign that her proud father had hidden under the carpet and she never failed to find it. She loved the applause from the party guests, but better still she was allowed to keep the coin.

Jack West's yard soon became well known for selling second-hand cars and spare parts. Now that the business was established he had a little spare time to indulge in a

170

hobby. Although he had given up racing motorcycles he still collected interesting models and could not resist making his own modifications. When he was a small boy he had been given a canary, which he treasured, and he was still fascinated by all types of birds. He built a large aviary in his yard and started collecting a variety of songbirds. He regularly visited a breeder in Warwickshire called Jim who had vast aviaries filled with hundreds of birds. On one occasion Jim showed him a special little bird that he had bred and handled since it was young and was very tame. It was a siskin, a small finch, more common in the north of England and Scotland. Jack took such a shine to the bird that he asked if he could buy it but Jim was reluctant to sell. However, after much haggling Jack made him an offer he could not refuse and triumphantly took the bird home to show Doreen and Sylvia. Although Doreen did not like to see birds in cages, Cecil, as Sylvia named him, was too precious to live in the large aviary at the yard, so they bought him an extra large cage and he stayed at Eden Drive.

It was not long before the little bird had struck up such an affinity with Jack that, when he entered the room, it would flap its wings and jump up and down excitedly. One day, Jack told Doreen to open the cage door to see what Cecil would do. So, after closing the windows, she unfastened the small door catch and stood to one side. Sure enough, Cecil flew straight to Jack and settled on his outstretched hand. After that he was trusted to leave his cage more and more. Doreen was about to serve dinner one evening, when she found Jack feeding tasty morsels of bird seed to Cecil, who was happily perched on his side plate.

"Jack! That's going too far. He'll make a mess on the table cloth."

Jack shook his head, "No he won't, he knows better than that." To their astonishment Cecil flew back to his cage, relieved himself, and then returned to his place on the dinner table. "I told you so," said Jack casually. Consequently, he was allowed to join the family at meal times, when an extra plate was laid for him, and he never once disgraced himself.

Spaniels are renowned to be gentle dogs and Spot accepted Cecil as part of the family, he would not have harmed the little bird even though he sometimes flew dangerously close. When guarding the house, however, he could become quite fierce as Wilf learnt to his cost. He called at the house one day and knocked on the door, but no one answered, although he thought Doreen was probably at home as the door was unlocked. He stepped inside, shouting a loud, "Hello!" to attract attention and was given a friendly welcome by Spot who was wagging his tail with excitement. There was still no answer to his call so he turned to go and was confronted with a very different dog as Spot stood between him and the door, growling and baring his teeth. When he made a move towards the door he was grabbed by his trouser leg and held firmly. Wilf was not afraid of dogs, he owned a lovely black labrador, but decided to let Spot have his own way and sat down to read a newspaper till help arrived. Jack was the first to return home and thought Wilf's predicament was hilarious. "That soft old thing wouldn't hurt a fly."

* * *

The country was in an optimistic and festive mood. After the sad death of George VI the forthcoming coronation of the young princess Elizabeth led to a feeling of hope for a bright future.

Doreen heard a rumour that there was to be a rehearsal for the procession a few days before the big event. Edith had come to stay for a week so, with Sylvia, they got up in the early hours of the morning and set out to pick up Louie on the way to London.

They arrived about six o'clock and after parking the car in a side street, walked to The Mall and waited. A scattering of people began to congregate along the route and it was evident they were not going to be disappointed when they heard the clatter of horses' hooves.

With the police in attendance, the cavalry rode by on their dark bay horses followed by the ceremonial coaches pulled by grey horses. The riders and coachmen were not in their full ceremonial dress but the coronation coach was a sight to be seen. After the procession had passed the four ladies wandered up to the palace gates with some of the other spectators and peered through, though apart from the guards there was little to be seen. Reluctantly, they made their way back to the car and headed for home.

The day of the coronation was spent gathered round the television. Nobody wanted to miss an instant of this rare spectacle and the young queen was greatly admired for the way she conducted herself throughout the long ceremony, her handsome husband by her side.

CHAPTER
SEVENTEEN

Sylvia had been given some riding lessons by a kind lady called Miss Ritchie, who lived locally, and in spite of some painful falls she was still horse mad. She had been saving all her pocket money in the vain hope of buying a pony. When asked what she would like for Birthday or Christmas presents the answer was always the same: "Some money for my Pony Box." This was a small biscuit tin which held her savings, but as ponies became more expensive she was never likely to get more than half way towards her goal. Doreen decided that now the salon was up and running they could afford to make up the difference and pay for all the additional extras.

She had heard of a dealer called Bill Williams who bought and sold horses and ponies of all descriptions. However, when Doreen and Sylvia visited him to see if he had a suitable pony, the only one small enough for Sylvia was very young, a bay gelding called Kadett. Though an older pony would have been more satisfactory, he was so pretty that a deal was struck. Bill fitted Kadett with a saddle and bridle and promised to deliver him the next day. They had arranged to rent a paddock nearby where he would have the company of another pony.

Neither Doreen or Sylvia slept much that night. When the ancient horse box arrived their excitement knew no bounds. Bill led the pony down the ramp and handed the halter rope to Sylvia. After making a fuss of him and feeding him carrots, she let him loose in the paddock and watched as he galloped off towards the other pony, tail in the air, rearing, bucking and showing off. That evening, armed with saddle, bridle and buckets of feed, they arrived at the paddock for her to have her first ride. Unfortunately, Kadett had other ideas, he was not going to be caught! They rattled the feed bucket and held out titbits, but he just galloped off taking his new friend with him. As darkness fell they went back to the car and Doreen felt sorry for Sylvia who had looked forward for so long to ride her very own pony.

"Let's get up early in the morning and try again," she said.

At first light they went back, only to find the naughty pony chasing his companion round the paddock and kicking out at him. The possibility of the other pony being hurt really worried them and they decided, as it was fairly certain they were not going to be able to catch the little rascal, they would contact Bill to see if he had any suggestions. After listening to their tale of woe, he had to agree that Kadett was not the right pony for Sylvia. He knew where there was a nice mare for sale that might suit her but, of course, a little more money would have to change hands!

Sparky was exchanged for the naughty Kadett and was a great success, Sylvia adored her. She was Sparky by name and Sparky by nature, a fast little pony, usually well mannered but if her mood changed she would buck her rider off in a flash. Sylvia soon made friends with other pony mad girls especially Diana Clifton, who lived quite near. In the school holidays the two girls were practically inseparable, more like sisters.

One day, Jack came home in a super new American car, a Fairlaine. "Shall we have a day out in it tomorrow?" he suggested. "I thought we could take Sylvia and Diana to London for a treat. We could go to Olympia to see Bertram Mills Circus? It'll be the last chance to have an outing for a while as I shall be working on the Fairlaine."

Doreen looked at him in disbelief. "Surely you don't have to repair it, it's new?"

"Left-hand drive cars are not worth so much in this country so I'm going to change it to a right-hand drive. At least, I'm going to try."

"But you'll have to alter everything," said Doreen, "steering wheel, pedals, instruments. It's impossible."

"Nothing's impossible and there's no such word as can't," he replied. It was not the first time he had taken on formidable tasks such as this and she knew that he would not rest until it was finished even if it meant missing meals and working late into the night.

They set off the next morning in high spirits and were soon in the West End of London to shop in the superb apartment stores. Jack treated them to a sumptuous lunch at The Savoy after which they made their way to Olympia where he had managed to get seats in the front row. The band struck up and the show began with hilarious antics from the clowns followed by graceful

176

liberty horses going through their paces, to the delight of Sylvia and Diana. Next came a troupe of elephants moving elegantly in single file, each one holding the tail of the one in front with its trunk. One of the lovely creatures broke rank and walked purposefully to the centre of the ring, giving the impression that he was going to perform a solo act. The audience waited expectantly, but his performance was obviously not rehearsed or expected. He lifted his tail, broke wind quite explosively and deposited a very large heap before calmly walking off to rejoin his comrades. Doreen was sure he had a grin on his face as he passed by. Before the laughter had subsided a very small man came running into the ring carrying an outsize shovel. It was evident he would be hard pressed to remove the heap all at once, but he had no intention of making two journeys and piled it onto the shovel with great expertise. One lump eluded him, however, so he picked it up with his fingers and placed it neatly on the top. By this time the audience were in fits of laughter and when he returned to the ring to take a bow the clapping was quite deafening until the ring master chased him out of sight.

The three girls dozed in the comfortable limousine as Jack drove them home late that night, they would always remember their fabulous day out.

Louie had become quite well known with the local estate agents and her morning post often contained particulars of houses for sale in the neighbourhood in the hope that they might tempt her to move yet again and bring off another sale.

As her mail dropped through the letter box, one cold wet day, amongst the usual buff envelopes was another letter from Henry. They were now corresponding quite regularly and as time had passed he sounded more optimistic. He wrote in such a friendly informative way with wonderful descriptions of Singapore, its lifestyle and countryside that she found his letters fascinating. This time, however, he told her that he would not now be coming back to England for some time as he was in the process of buying a house in Singapore where he could spend his retirement. Louie could not help feeling disappointed and realized that she had been looking forward to his return, now it seemed that she might never see him again.

Don and Wilf were at work and the house felt cold and empty so she decided to cheer herself up and telephoned Margaret to make an appointment to have her hair permed.

"I can fit you in after Mrs Nickerson at eleven o'clock," said Margaret.

When Louie arrived Margaret's appointments were running a little late. "I'm sorry to keep you waiting," she said, "but I've just wetted Mrs Nickerson's knickers." She then explained that her client had very long hair and when she was washing it, she had somehow lost control, swamping the unfortunate lady's lap.

Louie really enjoyed her morning in the busy little salon. A good chat and plenty of laughs, she was feeling better already! Between the comings and goings she told them that she had heard that there was to be a block of flats built on the lovely open piece of land by the side of her house.

"What a good excuse for a move," teased Doreen, winking at Margaret.

"You're right, I'm not staying there," Louie joined in the laughter. "Besides, the flats will keep the sunlight from my garden."

"Have you got anywhere in mind?" asked Margaret.

"I've seen a For Sale notice outside a house on Hernes Road, not far from where I live. I'm hoping Doreen might come with me to have a look at it."

"You must ask Margaret if I can have the time off," said Doreen. "I'm only the apprentice."

"I suppose I'll have to let you go," Margaret smiled as she held up the hand mirror for Louie to view her completed hairdo which met with instant approval.

The next day Louie and Doreen arrived outside the impressive house which stood on the corner of Hernes Road surrounded by a high wall. As they entered through a solid oak door in the wall they gasped when they caught sight of the most beautiful garden, it was like walking into paradise. A mulberry tree stood proud on the lawn and beyond it was a large goldfish pond with a fountain playing. There were borders of many flowering shrubs, ornamental stone troughs overflowed with fuchsias, geraniums and lobelia and statues of graceful naked ladies and other ornaments completed the peaceful scene. It was hard to believe that there was a busy main road just the other side of the wall. Louie loved gardening and Doreen knew there was hardly any need to look over the house, but as they stood in the spacious rooms with large windows overlooking such a vista, Louie was left in no doubt and they returned immediately to the estate agents office to make a definite offer.

Wilf called at Eden Drive on his way home from work.

"What did you think of Mother's new house?" Doreen asked.

"It's lovely, but I'm concerned about her trying to cope with all that gardening. Don and I will help all we can but I'll not be at home for much longer, Rosemary and I have set a date for our wedding."

Doreen hugged him. "Have you told Mother yet? She'll be so pleased."

"We're going to tell her this evening," he said. "We only decided yesterday."

Margaret, who had been sorting bundles of clean towels for the salon, joined them for a celebration drink.

The next weekend Rosemary and Wilf drove down to Wales to visit her grandfather. It was a bright sunny morning and when they arrived he was sitting in the garden apparently reading the newspaper, but really he had one eye on the road watching for their car. As they approached he was soon at the gate to greet them. Rosemary introduced him to her fiancé and the two men shook hands. There was an awkward silence and Wilf felt a little apprehensive as the old gentleman sized him up, then turning to his granddaughter he said, "He'll do. You look after him, my dear, and he'll last you a lifetime."

* * *

Cecil the siskin had become so tame that Jack frequently let him fly around in the house and he would return to his cage of his own accord. When, one day, he told Sylvia and Doreen he was going to let him fly outside they begged him not to.

"He won't know how to fend for himself," Doreen said, but he was sure he would come back and carried the little bird in his cage into the garden. Phil and May Morgan, who kept the grocery store next door, were intrigued as they watched over the garden fence. Jack opened the cage door. Cecil took to the skies and flew straight to some tall elm trees about a hundred yards away landing on the topmost branch. There was no doubt in anyone's mind they would never see him again. Doreen felt certain Jack was regretting his actions as he hung the cage on the side of the garage and optimistically propped open the door. There were tears in Sylvia's eyes as she ran indoors and Phil and May tactfully returned to stacking their shelves. Jack slowly walked to the dining room without a word and sat by the French window which overlooked the garden. Doreen was preparing lunch, although she suspected no one would have much appetite, and discreetly removed Cecil's plate from the table. She did not hear the door open and was completely taken aback when Jack came into the kitchen carrying the bird cage with Cecil happily sitting on the perch. She hastily popped the little bird's plate back on the table and Sylvia ran next door to tell Phil and May the good news.

"I hope you never do that again," said Doreen.

"Only when the weather's good."

"He's teasing," Doreen whispered to Sylvia, seeing the alarmed look on her face.

The next day was again warm and sunny so Jack came home early for his lunch to let Cecil have another little fly. This time it was not long before he returned to his cage and was soon lunching as usual with the family. Simmy had come to visit for the day and have her hair done and was highly amused at the antics of the tiny bird. The ritual was repeated every day for about a fortnight and Doreen and Sylvia were getting less anxious though always thankful when he was safely indoors. Then one day, after he had flown off a dark cloud appeared and quite suddenly there was a heavy downpour. It would be the first time in his life that Cecil had been out in the rain and it continued all afternoon. There was no sign of him and as darkness fell he still had not returned. Doreen could not sleep for thinking of him, by now he was probably cold, wet and hungry. She knew Jack was awake too but neither spoke. She had no sooner dozed off than she was woken by the dawn chorus and leapt out of bed. Not stopping to dress, she ran downstairs and into the garden where a morning mist had formed partially obscuring the cage but promising a fine day. She ran across the sodden lawn and could hardly believe her eyes. There, in the bottom of the cage, was Cecil pecking at his seed.

"Thank goodness you're back safe and sound," she said as she closed the door. In high spirits, she ran indoors to wake the family and tell them the good news.

"Please don't let him out again, Daddy," Sylvia pleaded and Jack promised he never would. So that was the end of Cecil's little jaunts outside.

182

Margaret was looking through the appointments book and found she had a spare slot so offered to shampoo and set Doreen's hair. Doreen eagerly accepted her offer, there was nothing she enjoyed more than having her hair done. She watched and admired Margaret's nimble fingers and began to doubt her own ability.

"Do you think I'll ever be a hairdresser?" she asked.

Margaret laughed. "You'll do," she said. "I'll have to leave soon anyway, I can't be changing nappies and styling hair so it's time for you to take over. I'm sure you'll manage."

The news came as a bombshell to Doreen. "It's wonderful news over the baby but whatever shall I do without you? I shall miss you terribly." She could not believe that two years had passed since Margaret had joined her in the salon. In spite of all the hard work it had been a happy time and they had had such fun together. They chatted non-stop about Margaret's baby plans until she handed Doreen a magazine and lowered the hair dryer over her head. Unable to concentrate on reading, she wondered how she was going to manage to run the salon on her own.

Louie had settled into her new home. With her two sons to keep her company she was very happy there in spite of having to get up at five o'clock in the morning to cope with the large garden. It would not be long however, before they would be leaving her to go their separate ways. She still exchanged letters with Henry regularly and enjoyed their correspondence but did not expect to see him in England again.

Olive and Jane continued to bring their friends from The Cedars. By now the servicemen had returned home but there were still many patients recovering from operations and illnesses who benefited from their practical help and outings in the Daimler. They kept the old car sparkling with polish, Jack looked after its mechanical welfare and it never let them down. Olive and Jane still shared the driving and there was always friendly rivalry over whose turn it was to take the wheel.

Louie loved planning their tea parties and when the weather was fine they could sit and relax by the fountain in her enchanting garden.

Wilf visited Doreen in high spirits to tell her of his new business venture. He had bought a garage in Headington where he could carry out repairs and the business also included four Daimler limousines which were used as hire cars for weddings and funerals. Adjoining the garage was a stone built cottage which, after a little loving care, would make a cosy home for Wilf and Rosemary after their marriage.

The day of the wedding arrived and the gleaming limousines were put to good use to transport bride, groom and guests in style to Wolvercote church. It was such a happy day, there could never have been a more handsome couple in spite of the fact that the groom had forgotten to shave! It was a lovely ceremony and Louie was moved to tears, she thought that Algy would have been very proud of their youngest son.

It was arranged that Don would chauffeur the newlyweds to the reception, but as he was closing their door he was distracted by the antics of one of the guests. Wilf grasped the door handle and pulled it to. It wouldn't shut so he gave it a harder slam. Don let out a scream. "My fingers!" He was helped onto the back seat of the car next to the bride, and the groom drove them post haste to the reception where a stiff drink was administered. This relieved his pain so effectively that he thought it would be a good idea to have another and another and by the end of the afternoon he had forgotten his pain altogether.

CHAPTER
EIGHTEEN

Sylvia asked her parents if she could take Sparky to a gymkhana which was to be held nearby at Barton. "It wouldn't be too far for me to ride there," she said. "All my friends are going."

Jack was always very busy at weekends and would not be able to go but Doreen said she would drive over in the car and pick Louie up on the way. Sylvia spent the following week practising some of the gymkhana events.

Early Saturday morning, with Sparky groomed to perfection, she set off with Miss Ritchie and Diana, who had borrowed a pony for the occasion. Doreen and Louie followed later with the car loaded with grooming kit, halters and horse food.

By the time they arrived there was quite a gathering of horses and riders, many of them local farmers and their children. The majority of competitors had hacked to the event, but parked in a neat row were six smart horseboxes, the owners of which had come from farther afield and their horses had travelled in luxury and arrived looking immaculate. One envious child on her woolly pony was heard to say, "I expect they're 'pot hunters'." Sylvia, however, gazed in awe and was determined that, one day, she would ride well enough to warrant a turnout like that!

She took part in three gymkhana events and, in spite of her practice sessions, she was unprepared for the speed and agility of the other competitors. "How can they go so fast?" she asked Diana who was equally taken aback. Their last event was the Pole Bending race and when the starter dropped his flag Sparky lit up and streaked between the poles turning so sharply at the other end that Sylvia nearly fell off, the pony had obviously done this before and to her great joy they won first prize. They were all very tired by the time they had ridden home and fed the ponies but she could not sleep that night. She had won her first rossette!

Margaret was going to leave the following week and Doreen was feeling a little apprehensive about coping with the salon on her own, so when she saw an advertisement in the *Oxford Mail* that a hairdresser was in search of employment, she replied immediately. A very smart young lady called Cheryl arrived for the interview who seemed to be well qualified and Doreen was so impressed that she arranged for her to come for a week's trial.

Sylvia's hair needed a trim and, as Doreen was busy with a customer, she asked if Cheryl could cut it and maybe give her a new hair style.

"Shall I give you a tulip cut?" she said enthusiastically as she pushed her into a chair, drew the curtain around the cubicle and tied a cape around her shoulders. As she brandished the scissors, Sylvia, who was by now feeling decidedly nervous, nodded in agreement although she had no idea what a tulip cut was. Then she watched in horror as her hair was snipped into a hideous shape. Doreen pulled aside the pink curtain and entered the cubicle to see how she was getting on. When she saw the state of her daughter's hair she was dumbfounded, not so much a tulip, more a ragged robin! Later, when she was alone with Cheryl, she questioned her more thoroughly and it transpired that she had been working as a clippie on the buses and the extent of her hairdressing skills were a couple of home perms. Not daring to let her perform tulip cuts on any of the customers, Doreen paid her a week's wages in lieu of notice and made up her mind to manage on her own.

Jack was very busy at his yard and had taken on a man to help him. Ted was a strong and willing worker, he had a quiet easy going manner and was polite with the customers. Jack noticed that his boots were in a sorry state and decided to buy him a new pair, he would have to guess his size. He was afraid that if he gave him the money to buy them himself it would more likely be spent in the off-licence than the shoe shop.

"Do you think these are your size, Ted?" he said, handing him the boots. "I thought you could do with some new ones."

Ted's face lit up. "Thanks Boss," he said. "I'm sure they'll fit, my feet be pretty pliable." He changed into the boots there and then and, judging by his broad smile, Jack thought they probably fitted his pliable feet quite well.

188

It was hard, dirty work and the saying, "where there's muck, there's money", was not entirely true, but it was a living. Jack liked to keep a quality car for his own use, usually a Jaguar, Rolls-Royce or Bentley. This, combined with his generous nature, always the first to buy a round of drinks, often gave colleagues the false impression that his business was very prosperous.

Doreen had gained her confidence in the everyday running of the salon and her clients seemed satisfied with her work. She was not looking forward, however, to her first attempt to style the hair of Margaret's star customer, Mrs Celia Houghton-Smythe. This imposing lady competed in ballroom dancing competitions with her husband and wore her hair in a swept up style decorated with ostrich feathers and diamanté. Doreen managed to concoct such an elaborate hairdo that she surprised even herself and was rewarded with a hefty tip. Mrs Houghton-Smythe became a regular customer and Doreen looked forward to her visits to learn how she had fared in her latest competitions.

Mrs Nickerson continued to come to the salon and, like Margaret, on her first attempt Doreen found it difficult to wash her long hair without swamping the poor lady. As she was rather short Doreen put some cushions on her chair to raise her nearer to the level of the basin and she found that this helped no end. She insisted that her hair should be crimped into waves at the top but by the time the rest of it had been dried most of the intricate styling had been pulled straight. Doreen was not happy with the result but the lady seemed satisfied and she also continued to be a regular customer.

189

When she was not at school Sylvia's time was devoted to Sparky. As well as riding around the countryside with her friends she spent many hours grooming and riding in the field on her own. "I wish you could ride with me, Mummy," she would often say, and though Doreen would loved to have joined her, it seemed out of the question.

A young lady called Karen came into the salon for a shampoo and set and Doreen remembered having met her before. She sometimes rode out with Sylvia on a pony called Champ. The pony was an attractive strawberry roan colour and though quite thickset had a pretty little head with a permanent smile. Sylvia had often remarked how well-behaved he was. During their conversation Doreen learned that she was soon going to college and was going to have to part with him.

"Do you know anyone who might buy Champ?" she said. "I want him to go to a good home."

"Would you sell him to me?" asked Doreen on the spur of the moment. "I couldn't afford to pay much but I'd look after him well and I'd love to have him."

Karen was overjoyed and a deal was struck with the proviso that she could visit him whenever she liked and ride him in her holidays.

It was not long before Champ had taken up residence in the paddock with Sparky and they became the best of friends. Doreen was looking forward to her first ride on him with a little trepidation as she had not ridden since she was twelve years old when she lived at Mill Farm, Black Bourton. However, she told herself that it must be like riding a bike, you never quite forget!

The last customer had left and she closed the salon door. It had been a hard day and her back was aching but she was too excited to let a little thing like that prevent her trying out her new pony. It was not long before she was mounted and happily riding round the paddock. The dear pony seemed to sense the situation and kept to a walk. Doreen though feeling less nervous by the minute was thankful for his consideration. She could not believe her luck in finding such a suitable pony.

After a couple of weeks she had gained her confidence and was riding out with Sylvia and enjoying every minute. The fun they had with these two small ponies led them on to a greater involvement with horses which lasted for many years to come.

Don and Evelyn were making plans for their wedding and, to Sylvia's delight, had asked her to be their bridesmaid. It was to be held at a church in Cowley near to Evelyn's home. They had bought a nice house in Horspath, a village close to Oxford and only a mile away from the famous Cowley factory where Morris cars were manufactured.

On the morning of the wedding Don woke early with a dreadful hangover, the result of a stag night drinking party the evening before. He took some aspirin and began to feel a little better. The sun was shining and he decided that the best thing to clear his head would be to have a ride on his motorbike. Louie was still asleep so he crept out of the house and didn't start the machine until he had pushed it a short distance down the road. He headed towards Henley, then turned off in Nettlebed onto a country lane which led to the Chiltern Hills. Speeding along with the wind in his hair, he was not only feeling better but on top of the world. The sun was shining, the purr of his Norton's powerful engine was music to his ears and later he was going to marry the girl he loved.

Then he heard the engine splutter again and again until it lost power and stopped. When he looked at the fuel gauge the needle was on empty. *How could I have been so stupid not to have checked it before I left?* he thought. He looked around but there were no houses in sight so he would just have to push the heavy machine till he could find a telephone box. He walked on for miles and was feeling exhausted in the heat of the sun. A farmhouse came into view and his spirits rose.

A man was opening the gate into the yard and spotted Don. "It looks as if you've got a bit of trouble, lad," he said.

"Could I use your phone please. I've run out of petrol?"

"We don't have no phone," he answered. "Don't have no need for one."

"Oh dear," said Don. "Where's the nearest petrol pump? I'm getting married this afternoon and I shall never get back to Oxford in time."

"We can't have you being late for your wedding," laughed the farmer. "The nearest pump is in Stokenchurch. If we can lift your bike into my old van I'll drive you there."

They managed to heave the heavy machine into the van and secured it with some rope.

"Get in, lad," he said as he climbed into the driving seat. Before Don could close the door three dogs and a cat had pushed their way in with him. "You won't have to mind them, they like a ride out."

It was not long before the van had chugged its way to Stokenchurch. Don was so grateful for the farmer's help and wanted to pay him for his trouble but he would have none of it and jumped into the van and started the engine. "Just you hurry up and get to the church, lad. Don't keep your lady waiting," he shouted as he drove off.

With a full tank of petrol Don raced for home. As he neared Oxford on a good straight road he realized that he was travelling at ninety miles an hour and hoped that there were no police cars around.

He reached home with only minutes to spare before his wedding appointment.

"Where have you been?" Louie was furious. "How could you be so irresponsible? We were so worried about you."

Wilf, who was to be best man, was waiting to take him to the church and whisked him away as soon as he had changed his clothes but they were still twenty minutes late. The bride's car had to drive around the block several times before the groom appeared. Evelyn was so relieved to see Don safe and sound that she soon forgave him for his tardiness when she learnt what had happened. She looked lovely in her white brocade dress and Sylvia, dressed in pink taffeta, overcame her shyness to enjoy her role as bridesmaid.

After their honeymoon in Shoreham, the bride and groom's first outing was to find the farmer in the Chilterns who had saved their wedding day. They took him some wedding cake, a bottle of whiskey and a big hug from the bride.

Louie was missing Don and Wilf more than she cared to admit and though Sylvia spent her school lunch hour with her it was a long day on her own. There was always plenty to do in the garden and weather permitting, Sylvia enjoyed helping her with the weeding and pushing the mower round the lawn. She loved feeding the goldfish, watching them come from their hiding places under the water lily leaves to grab their food.

Louie loved her home. It was a beautiful house with large rooms and high ceilings which made the most of her furniture and ornaments. Through the summer months she felt that there was nowhere else she would rather be. In winter, however, the house had a drawback, it always felt cold. No matter how much Louie stoked the boiler or piled coal onto the fires, the heat seemed to disappear up to the lofty ceilings.

She took to wearing extra jumpers, scarves and woolly socks. Doreen couldn't resist teasing her. "It looks as if you're off on an expedition to the Antarctic."

Even inviting guests for a meal had become an embarrassment as she watched them bolt their food so that they could leave the table to huddle near to the fire. It was going to be a difficult problem to solve before another winter without incurring considerable expense.

CHAPTER
NINETEEN

Joan and Percy had bought a bungalow called Wayside with about two acres of land which was situated near the village of Cassington. Though the entrance was on the busy Oxford to Witney road, it was in an isolated spot at the end of a long drive. Percy was the manager of a large Oxford garage and he planned to run a poultry farm as a sideline. They soon had it decorated throughout and the garden abounding with flowers and shrubs. Most of the land was divided into chicken runs and they constructed a large building to house the hens on deep litter in the winter.

Doreen and Jack took Louie to visit them one evening and were met in the garden by Percy who was carrying baskets of large brown eggs. At his heels were two bull mastiff dogs, Penny and Beauty, which he had bought to keep Joan company while he was at work. Jack jumped back as Penny gave a defensive growl but Beauty was soon welcoming him by licking his face. Percy laughed. "A fat lot of good she is as a guard. She loves everybody."

Doreen watched Louie with amusement as she studied the contents of the baskets intently. Percy proudly showed them around the property and after helping to pack the eggs into boxes they sat by a cosy log fire for a drink and a chat.

The next day Louie received a letter from an old friend, Gwen, who was the widow of Algy's former bank manager, David Trent. After her husband died, she and her young son, Jason, went to live in Hove. Though they had corresponded regularly they had not seen each other for years and Gwen had written to invite Louie to stay for a few days. She accepted the invitation and boarded the train to Brighton a week later.

Gwen had promised to meet her at the station, but when she stepped onto the platform she could not see anyone who resembled her friend. A couple approached her and introduced themselves as Gwen and Jason but she would never have recognized them. The small boy she remembered was now a tall handsome young man and his mother, who had been a lady of ample proportions, had lost so much weight that she was positively thin. Jason took Louie's suitcase and led them out of the station to his smart car and they soon arrived at their lovely home just a short distance from the sea front. Louie would never forget the spectacle of the garden which abounded with large pink and blue hydrangeas in full bloom.

They had so much news to catch up on that the afternoon flew by. The generous glass of sherry that Jason had poured for Louie was beginning to make her feel rather light-headed. She had not eaten since breakfast so she was delighted when Gwen suggested they have tea.

"We have a high tea about this time of day and that saves us bothering with supper later on," she said. "Do you like sardines?"

Louie nodded. "Yes thank you, Gwen. I'm partial to fish and, as you may remember, I've always got a good appetite."

Jason opened the sardine tin with a flourish while Gwen cut some thin slices of bread. After toasting the bread she cut off the crusts and smeared it with a little butter. She tossed the crusts out of the window for the birds and placed the toast on bone china plates, one slice each for Louie and herself and two slices for Jason. She cut the tiny fish through the middle and arranged them fastidiously on the toast. They soon disposed of the dainty dish and Louie waited expectantly hoping there might be a substantial pudding to make up for the shortcomings of the first course, but when Gwen cleared away the plates and brought a cup of coffee, she knew she was going to be disappointed. She watched enviously as a seagull flew past the window clutching a crust.

"Shall we take a walk," Gwen suggested. "It's nice to get some exercise after a meal."

As they wandered along the sea front arm in arm, Louie was aware of a mouth watering aroma coming from the local fish and chip shop. "That smells nice," she ventured but Gwen ignored the remark and walked on.

They spent the evening reminiscing until Jason returned after meeting friends at his local pub. He was happy and relaxed and Louie suspected that he had probably topped up his inadequate high tea with something more substantial from the bar. He bore no resemblance to his father's looks but had inherited his genial personality and sense of humour. No more sustenance was offered so it was time for bed.

In the privacy of her bedroom she searched in her handbag for something to eat but aspirins were all she could find so in desperation she swallowed a couple with a tooth mug full of water. *Unless things improve tomorrow I shall have to make an excuse and go home*, she thought.

A knock on her door woke her the next morning and Jason brought her a cup of tea. She was dazzled by the sun shining through her window. "Breakfast is ready when you are," he said. "It looks like being a nice day."

"It certainly does," Louie replied. She was washed, dressed and sitting at the table in no time for a breakfast of corn flakes. "You've been so kind to invite me here," she said. "I wondered if I could take you out to dinner this evening as a thank you for your generosity? The George Hotel just down the road looked nice, or wherever you recommend."

Gwen and Jason readily accepted her offer and said The George would be fine.

While exploring the town and shopping for gifts to take back for the family, Louie managed to buy chocolates and biscuits which she secreted in her handbag to keep at bay any future hunger pains.

The George Hotel provided an excellent menu and, to her astonishment, Gwen and Jason munched their way through four courses without leaving so much as a crumb on their plates. Louie didn't begrudge the hefty bill, in fact she was delighted that they obviously relished their meal, but she could not understand how they survived on such small rations at home. That night she slept well with a full stomach.

After a couple more days it was time for Louie to trundle her way home on the train. She had really enjoyed her seaside break. Gwen and Jason had been excellent company and had taken her on trips to Brighton and local places of interest which she had very much appreciated. They promised to come to Oxford for a holiday and stay with her and she looked forward to the opportunity of repaying their hospitality.

Joan was on her way to feed the hens one morning, when she heard the neighbouring farmer's old tractor come racing up the drive.

"Have you lost one of your dogs, Mrs Eadle?" he shouted breathlessly.

Joan called to them, but only Penny came running and she seemed upset.

"I was the far side of the field next to the lay-by tending to my sheep," he said. "I saw a lorry driver feeding a dog like yours and then he lifted it into his cab and drove off. I was too far away to get his registration number. I'm ever so sorry."

"Don't be sorry, Tom. You did your best and thank you for your trouble," said Joan. "I'll phone the police but I doubt there's anything they can do."

Ten days had gone by and they had given up hope of seeing Beauty again when the telephone rang and a policeman from High Wycombe told Joan that a bull mastiff dog had been found wandering on a busy road and handed into the station. She called to Robin and they jumped into her car and sped to High Wycombe where they were reunited with a thin, bedraggled foundling that was Beauty, though no longer beautiful.

After a bath and a lot of loving care she soon looked as good as ever, though she was less enthusiastic when welcoming strangers and never ventured onto the main road. Penny was so glad to have her back that she never left her side.

It was a hot summer's day and Louie was dozing in a deck chair under the trailing branches of the mulberry tree. She had been working hard all morning in the garden and her body ached. She did not hear the garden door open and was startled by a voice behind her.

"How are you, Spotlight Lou?" It was Percy. "Joan and I wondered if you'd like a ride out in the car and a drink in a country pub, though you look so comfortable here it seems a shame to drag you away."

"It's lovely to see you," she said. "Why don't you join me under my tree and I'll fetch some cool drinks."

They lazed for the rest of the afternoon, idly chatting and sipping long cold drinks of Pimms.

"I think your garden is glorious," said Joan. "We're moving to a house with a nice garden, though it would never compare to yours."

"Surely you're not leaving your lovely bungalow?" Louie was astonished. "What about your chickens? I thought you were settled there for life."

200

"Well, Joan hankers to get back to Oxford and by the time I get home from work I'm too tired to spend enough time with the hens," said Percy. "I must admit I shall miss the place. Perhaps when I retire I might be able to find somewhere else like Wayside."

Louie lay awake that night, tossing and turning. She could not help thinking about Joan and Percy's beautiful bungalow and how she wished she could live in the country again and keep chickens. *Those were such lovely brown eggs!*

Very early next morning, she telephoned Percy. "Would you sell Wayside to me?" she asked. "I'd love to live there."

"Of course you can have it if you want it, but you'd better come and have a good look round first," he said. "I'll come and fetch you tomorrow and give you a guided tour."

"That would be great," said Louie. "Don't sell it to anyone else in the meantime."

As they drove to Cassington the next day Louie had already made up her mind that she was going to buy Wayside. If she could run the poultry farm successfully it might provide her with an income. It would be lovely to live in a bungalow and no longer have to cope with stairs and she preferred the peace and quiet of the countryside and the fresh air. All she could think of were the bonuses of living there and if there were any drawbacks she would overcome them.

A deal was struck that included the poultry and Louie could not contain her excitement. Now she had to tell the rest of the family and she was not sure that they would approve. She telephoned Doreen that evening to tell her the news.

"It's a lovely place, Mother," she said, "but I don't think you should be living there on your own. It's too isolated. What if you had an accident or needed help? I shall worry about you."

Louie laughed. "I've got a telephone and it's not that far from the main road."

"It's a long way from the shops," said Doreen. "I can drive you to Oxford on my afternoon off but you're not going to find it very convenient."

"I can cycle to the local village shop and if there's a problem I can always take up driving again." Louie was resolute. "It's no good trying to change my mind. I've really fallen in love with the place and I can't wait to move in."

"Well, it's obvious your heart's set on it and if you think you'll be happy there, I'll do my best to help," said Doreen.

Louie's lovely house sold as soon as she put it on the market. A professor from Keble College in Oxford bought it because it was convenient for his work but mostly because he wanted to own that beautiful garden.

The first morning in her new home at Wayside, Louie was woken at five o'clock by a noisy cockerel crowing. She didn't mind and just lay in bed listening to the country sounds and planning her busy day. *At last, I really feel at home*, she thought.

Jack had decided to take up pigeon racing. He built a loft beside his aviary and with the help of some knowledgeable friends had bought some birds with first-class pedigrees to breed good racing stock. It was going to be a lengthy process, but as one of his mentors said, "Rome wasn't built in a day." He joined the local Pigeon Racing Club and after attending his first meeting was even more enthusiastic. He was now a member of the "flat cap brigade", as they were known, though he had never worn a cap in his life and was never likely to. He bought a special clock that was cleverly devised to register the time of the pigeon's return to the loft. The bird's racing ring was removed from its leg and placed in a small metal thimble which, when pushed into the device, punched out the time. Before a race all the competitors would meet to synchronize their clocks and have a drink or two.

The pigeons had settled down well and were now being let out of the loft every day for a fly round. It was time to start training two or three for their first race. As Jack intended to enter them for races where they were set free at venues in the south of England and eventually from France the birds had to be taken on short practice trips in that direction. Doreen volunteered to take them in her car so that Jack could wait by the loft for their return and time their progress. She mostly released them on the Lambourn Downs where they had a clear skyline. After she set them free they would soar high into the air, circle twice and then head straight for home. They were fascinating to watch and Doreen marvelled at the ability of these small birds to fly such long distances and know which way to go, a mystery which has never been solved.

Some pigeon owners who did not own a car strapped their travelling baskets onto their bicycles for short trips and their birds usually returned to the lofts before them. For longer trips they sent the pigeons by rail and arranged for the station master at their destination to release them at a certain time so that their pace could be assessed. Jack's pigeons, however, usually rode with Sylvia on the back seat of Doreen's car. Louie often joined them on these trips for a ride out and an excuse for a picnic.

Out of the three birds that Jack was training, one blue cock always arrived home first but there was a problem. On a race day it was essential that the pigeon went straight inside the loft so that Jack could catch it and remove its racing ring. This chap, however, would sprint home only to sit on the roof for hours and nothing would tempt it inside. The other two hens always entered the loft immediately on their return and Jack found it frustrating to have such a fast pigeon that was going to be useless unless it changed its ways.

The time had come to enter the two well-behaved birds for their first race. Very early in the morning, the competitors gathered in Oxford to load their pigeons onto a train to take them to Bournemouth. Jack spent the morning working to take his mind off the waiting, even the fastest birds would not return home until early afternoon. At midday however, the skies began to cloud over and it became very dark, culminating in the most horrendous storm. There were high winds, thunder and heavy rain, none of which had been forecast. Two hours later the storm had passed and the sun was shining.

It was time to start looking out for the birds and Jack, Doreen and Sylvia took up positions in comfy chairs where they could watch the skies. The afternoon dragged on and still no sign of them and their cheerful optimism began to wane, they had not expected the birds to win any prizes, they just wanted them home safe and sound. It was getting dark and Doreen and Sylvia went home but Jack said he would wait a little longer. In fact, he did not return for another two hours. Doreen could tell by the look on his face that there was no sign of his pigeons.

When he went to the club meeting that evening there was a sombre atmosphere as only a quarter of the birds had returned. The storm must have caused the tragedy and no one could remember so many losses in one race, although they all hoped that some of the birds might still come home eventually. There were so many hazards to beset racing pigeons: storms, birds of prey, power lines and some owners even accused farmers of shooting them in mistake for the wild variety that plundered their newly sown corn.

"Poor old Jack," said Andrew, one of the members who had made him welcome when he first joined the club. "What a thing to happen on your maiden race. You'll be getting the impression that this racing lark is not the fun it's cracked-up to be."

"Well, I was wondering whether I could ever go through that again. I'm really fond of those birds," said Jack. "I think the best thing is for me to buy a round of drinks to toast the winners and the rest of us can drown our sorrows."

Every morning for a week he rose early to check the loft for arrivals but they never returned.

"There are three young birds ready to start training," said Doreen. "Shall I take them out tomorrow. We might as well put that awkward one in the basket as well." Jack had obviously lost heart but with a little encouragement from his family he caught and loaded the birds for their trip the next day. On Doreen's return she found Jack in high spirits. All four birds had come home safely and the blue cock was not only very fast but had entered the loft immediately. On subsequent training sessions he always came back quickly but could still be reluctant to pass through the trap door. He liked to keep Jack on tenterhooks. *Will he or won't he?* Thus he earned himself the nickname, Willy.

Willy was entered for his first race and came home so fast that Jack could not believe it when Doreen spotted the little bird winging its way to the loft. It dropped down and was through the trap door in a flash. With his ring safely in the clock, Jack was thrilled. "This is nearly as good as racing round The Isle of Man!"

At the Pigeon Club meeting that evening, after all the clocks had been handed in, Willy was declared the winner of his race in a surprisingly fast time. Jack got on well with the other members and it was a popular win, the first of many that he was to have over the years. He improved his breeding stock and built up a very competitive loft. Willy went on to win more races but on the odd occasion he would taunt his keeper by sitting on the loft roof for hours and refuse to be clocked in. When Jack found it difficult not to lose his temper, he would think back to that first sad race and just be thankful that the rascal was home safe and sound.

CHAPTER
TWENTY

Louie's telephone rang one sunny morning.

"I wondered if you'd like a ride out this afternoon?" Doreen's voice sounded chirpy. "I've got to drive to Milton Common to meet a delivery lorry that's coming from London and then the driver can follow me to Jack's yard so that he doesn't get lost."

"I'd love to come," said Louie. "What time shall I be ready?"

"About one o'clock. Jack's bought an elephant. Must dash!" The telephone clicked off and Doreen had gone.

Well, thought Louie, *it looks like being an interesting afternoon.*

As they drove towards the meeting place Louie couldn't contain her curiosity. "Did you mention an elephant?"

"That's right," said Doreen. "Jack sometimes goes to a nightclub in London with his friend, George. When they were there last night he met a chap who had an elephant for sale. After a drink or two, he bought it. Of course, it's not a live one, it's mechanical. Apparently there are only two in this country and the other one belongs to Terry Thomas, the actor."

As they drove into the car park of The Three Pigeons public house they saw a large flatbed lorry surrounded by a group of onlookers. Towering above them was a magnificent full sized elephant. It was stunningly lifelike.

Doreen bought the driver, Stan, a drink and a snack and then drove slowly ahead of the lorry down the winding country lanes to Jack's yard. She and Louie watched with amusement at the reactions of people that they passed as they caught sight of the elephant. One cyclist actually fell off his bicycle as he turned to get a better look.

Jack had been anxiously looking out for them. He had only seen a photograph of his purchase and was having second thoughts. *Maybe this elephant deal was not such a good idea after all?* As he directed the driver where to park, however, he was delighted, it was even better than he had hoped. The previous owner had told him that the elephant had a Ford car engine, complete with log book, and was taxed to use on the highway. When propelled by the engine it strode rather than rolled and would carry several passengers.

"How are you going to get it off my lorry then, Guvnor?" asked Stan.

"I don't know. How did you get it on there?" Jack replied.

"We had a crane."

"Well I haven't got a crane." Then Jack had a brainwave. "I think my flatbed lorry is the same height as yours. If we back them up together we might be able to drive it across onto mine."

They manoeuvred the lorries into place and Jack managed to haul himself onto the elephant's back. He started the engine and when he put it into gear it lurched forward and with lumbering strides made its way onto the other vehicle. To Jack's relief, when he applied the brakes it stopped.

"Phew, there's not many people can say they've driven an elephant," he said as he clambered down.

The lorry driver was unimpressed, just thankful to be rid of his load so that he could set out on his homeward journey.

That night Jack was tossing and turning in bed.

"I suppose you're puzzling how to get that elephant down from your lorry," Doreen laughed. "Sylvia and I were looking forward to having a ride on it but it's no good stuck up there."

"I didn't buy it for you to go gadding about," he said. "I thought I could make some money by hiring it out. An unusual thing like that has got to stir up some publicity, it could have all sorts of uses."

"It's no good trying to sound so self-righteous," said Doreen. "We both know that the only reason you bought it was because you'd had a few drinks, but with a bit of luck it might be a money spinner if you ever find a way of unloading it."

"Oh, I'll think of something," he said.

When Ted arrived for work the next morning he stopped in his tracks and stared in amazement when he saw the elephant.

"What's that then, Boss?"

"What's what, Ted?" Jack was busy changing a radiator on a Morris Eight.

"Well, it looks like an elephant standing on your lorry."
Ted lifted his greasy old cap and scratched his head.

His employer peered out from under the car bonnet,
"So it does."

"How did it get there then?"

"Darned if I know."

Ted wandered off mumbling, "I'm glad it's not pink or
I might've had to cut down on the booze."

A month later the elephant still stood proud, looking
out over the yard like a large statue. It was very popular
with his customers who would return again and again on
the pretext of buying some small part for their car so that
they could bring their family to view this unusual
spectacle. Pressure of work meant that Jack had had little
time to find a way of moving it.

George telephoned him one afternoon. "Isn't it time
we had a night out? I know you're busy but a break
would do you good."

"Oh, all right then. I'll try and get finished early this
evening."

By eight o'clock the two pals were dressed in their
best and gliding up to London in Jack's smart old
Bentley. When they reached the night-club the barman
pointed to a man sitting on his own at a table. "That's Mr
Crombie and he's been asking to meet you, Mr West."

Intrigued, Jack introduced himself to the stranger who
invited him and George to share his table and have a
drink. It transpired that he had been trying to bring off a
deal with his friend to buy the elephant when Jack,
unknowingly, stepped in and beat him to it. He wanted it
to advertise his new London store and was so

disappointed on losing such a unique object that he was now prepared to pay more. After a few more drinks and a tempting offer, Mr Crombie managed to persuade Jack to part with it.

Stan arrived with his lorry a week later to collect the elephant. "You never did get it down then," he remarked.

"Just as well," Jack replied. "Because we would've had to get it back up again."

The elephant was simply reversed from one lorry to the other and on its way to London in no time. Jack felt a small pang of disappointment as it left. *Perhaps I shouldn't have sold it? We could've had some fun with it if I'd ever got it off the lorry.*

Louie was pedalling her bicycle home from the village post office. She was still exchanging letters with Henry regularly and had sent him some photographs of Wayside and her poultry enterprise. She was in quite a hurry as Wilf and Rosemary were coming to tea and she intended to spend the rest of the morning baking cakes. She spotted a kestrel hovering overhead, then it swooped onto a telegraph pole just ahead of her. As she drew near it flew to the next pole and appeared to be teasing her. She was so intrigued with the fascinating bird that she failed to notice a pot hole in the road and hit it with a bang. She was thrown forward and landed on the grassy bank. Sitting for a while to get her breath back, she was relieved to find that she didn't seem to be hurt but when she picked up the bicycle to continue on her way she discovered that the front wheel was badly buckled. She still had a fair distance to go but would just have to drag it the rest of the way. The kestrel circled above her then swooped once more before flying away.

The wheel was making a clanking noise as she trudged along. A lorry passed her, then slowed up and reversed back towards her. The driver jumped out of his cab.

"Can I give you a lift?" he said. "Looks as if your old bike's let you down."

"That would be kind of you," she said. "My shoulders were beginning to ache."

He lifted her bicycle onto the back of his lorry then opened the passenger door for her. The cab was set up high over the large front wheels and Louie had difficulty climbing in, but she managed to grasp a handle and pulled herself the rest of the way. He started the powerful noisy engine and off they went. *This is fun*, she thought. From her lofty seat she had a wonderful view through the large windscreen. They reached Wayside in no time and the driver unloaded her bicycle.

"I've enjoyed riding in your lorry," Louie said.

"Always glad to help a damsel in distress," he laughed. "Living out here it must be difficult sometimes. If you ever need a lift you'll find that most of us lorry drivers enjoy the company of a hitchhiker."

She gave him a drink and a box of new laid eggs and he went on his way.

When Rosemary and Wilf arrived they were positively glowing with happiness and couldn't wait to tell Louie their good news. Rosemary was expecting a baby, which was due in November.

While they were celebrating with a drink Wilf told his mother that a lucky opportunity had come their way. A new dual carriageway was to be built in Headington which was to turn a minor road into a major traffic route around Oxford. It was to run alongside their property and he had applied for planning permission to build a large forecourt for petrol pumps and a car showroom. If all went well they could soon be the proud owners of a substantial business on a prime site.

Two months later they heard that planning permission had been granted and Wilf set to work on laying out his new forecourt. It was very hard but rewarding work. Had the new road been scheduled to run slightly closer to Oxford it would have come straight through their property and they would have lost their business and home.

Louie's poultry farm was doing well. She had doubled the number of laying hens and was rearing chicks to replace them when they were past their prime for egg production. She bought in fertile eggs and hatched them in a large incubator. The chicks were then transferred to a brooder until they were strong enough to survive without extra heating. It was time consuming work but Louie enjoyed every minute. The experience she had gained when looking after the poultry on Algy's farm was now proving invaluable. She had also acquired some Khaki Campbell ducks. These were jolly little characters who ran around in the paddocks all day scavenging for juicy titbits and proved to be excellent layers. A trio of geese grazed the grassy paths and weeded between the vegetables. They would raise the alarm by cackling loudly if there were any strangers about and Louie loved to show off their enormous eggs when they laid in early spring, these made deliciously large omelettes and added richness to a cake mix. All her lovely fresh eggs sold well and the duck eggs were especially popular.

Next to Louie's land was a disused gravel pit which was used as a fishing lake. She would sometimes chat to the fishermen over the fence and quite often a fish was exchanged for a box or two of eggs. She could clean and gut a fish in no time, another skill learnt on the farm. With fresh vegetables from the garden and no shortage of chicken or duck to eat she lived well and cheaply.

In spite of being out in all weathers Louie loved her lifestyle at Wayside and was proud of what she had achieved. She was not lonely but loved to entertain visitors especially when Jane and Olive brought their friends from the convalescent home. They arrived one afternoon with a frail elderly lady called Gladys Reeves and a dapper little man called Freddie Frost. Although unsteady on his feet after a major operation, Freddie was a charmer. As they were chatting after tea they learnt that he was in the antiques business and seemed to be quite an authority. He was admiring Louie's silver tea urn and she told him that it had belonged to her grandfather. It had been given to him and her grandmother as a wedding present and as they were driving home from the ceremony near Stokenchurch, with the pony and trap laden with gifts, they were set upon by a highwayman. As he tried to grab the valuables, however, her grandfather beat him off with his whip and they galloped home to safety leaving the thief with a sore head.

Louie also showed Freddie some gold coins which she kept in a drawer in the sideboard. There were some gold sovereigns and a two pound piece which he said could be quite valuable and advised her to keep them as an investment. He was very helpful and Olive asked if he could look around her house to advise her on the value of some family silverware. Freddie said he would be glad to be of any assistance.

Doreen had recently bought a new horse called Tregorro but had had an unfortunate fall and landed awkwardly. She suffered a fractured spine and had just spent a fortnight in hospital. She was now home with her back supported in a plaster cast. It was a very painful injury and though she was now walking unaided it would be a long time before she was fully recovered. Her main concern was for her clients as she had had to close the salon. It would have been difficult to find a qualified hairdresser at short notice and Margaret's time was now devoted to her lovely baby girl, Marilyn. Doreen was going to have to think about her future as a hairdresser as it was a back aching occupation even for a fit person.

Louie wanted to go to Oxford to do some shopping. She needed some curtain material and knew that Webbers in the High Street was the most likely store to stock the pattern she was looking for. She didn't want to bother

Doreen for a lift as, although she was now out of plaster, she knew it was still painful for her to drive the car. She could afford to hire a taxi, though she would have to sell a lot of eggs to pay the fare, so decided against it. She remembered the friendly lorry driver who had given her a lift and thought she might wander down to the lay-by on the main road and see if there were any lorries parked there. She put on her smart coat and hat and, armed with a large shopping bag and a basket, she set off. As she neared the lay-by a furniture van pulled in. The driver wound down his window for some fresh air and Louie plucked up courage and walked round to his door.

"I wondered if you're going towards Oxford? Is there a chance of a lift?" she asked nervously.

"I'm going into the centre of Oxford to deliver some furniture," he said. "You're welcome to ride along. I'll be off in a minute when I've had a drink. Hop in." He produced a large Thermos flask and poured himself a mug of tea.

Louie hauled herself up into the passenger seat and they were soon on their way.

"How are you going to get home?" the driver asked as he carefully steered the large vehicle between the busy Oxford traffic. "I'll be about an hour unloading this lot in George Street and then I can give you a lift back if you've finished your shopping."

"That would be wonderful. An hour will give me plenty of time." She had been so intent on getting into Oxford that she had failed to plan her homeward journey.

When Louie arrived home later that afternoon she was feeling quite pleased with herself after a successful day. She had really enjoyed her trip in the lorry with the kind driver and had found some lovely curtain material, she even had a little time to wander round the stores. She had been extremely lucky today to find a driver who offered to bring her home but if she hitchhiked into Oxford again she would probably have to take a bus to the outskirts of town to find a lift back. She decided not to tell anyone about her new mode of transport as she didn't think the family would approve.

During one of their frequent telephone conversations Doreen asked Louie if she needed anything special from the shops that she could not buy locally. "My back's a lot better now and if you want to go to Oxford or Witney it's no trouble for me to drive you there. Now I'm not working in the salon I've plenty of spare time."

"I don't seem to need anything, it's amazing what you can buy in our village shop," Louie remarked casually and quickly changed the subject. "Will you be able to take up your hairdressing again?"

"Although my back is on the mend I don't think I'm going to be strong enough to work the long hours I spent in the salon. Though it was very tiring, I thoroughly enjoyed it and I shall miss seeing my regular customers," said Doreen, "but I'm going to have to sell up and look for somewhere else to live."

"What a pity to have to give up the business when it was running so well but I think it does you good to move house and have a change. It's never done me any harm and I've lost count of the number of houses I've owned," laughed Louie. "In fact, Mr Rose told me that when he can't sleep instead of counting sheep he tries to remember the many homes that I've lived in and falls asleep in no time."

CHAPTER
TWENTY-ONE

Doreen put the salon on the market and soon had a prospective buyer who intended to run it as a butcher's shop. He was anxious to move in as soon as possible. Although she had contacted all the local estate agents and had viewed several properties, she could not find anywhere that appealed to herself, Jack or Sylvia. She received some particulars one morning concerning a property in Old Marston which was only half a mile from Eden Drive. It was called Halford House but when she read the details it had no main water or drainage and was in a dilapidated condition so she thought no more about it as there would have been no time to make it habitable before moving in.

A few weeks later Joan telephoned her to see how the house hunting was progressing. "Did you ever go to see Halford House?" she asked.

"No. It looked awful on the particulars," said Doreen.

"Well, I think you ought to have a look at it. It's in a nice area. Let's go this afternoon." Joan was adamant.

The three storey stone house stood at the end of a quiet lane and had not been lived in for some time. It had a sheltered garden, large orchard and vegetable garden, but what really caught Doreen's eye was the farmyard with pig sties, stables, garages and a large stone barn. Next to the barn stood a small shed which contained an earth closet which was the one and only toilet facility.

They wandered around in the house where they found a well just inside the back door with a hand pump to fill the water tank in the attic. "I bet that's hard work," laughed Doreen. "But I suppose it would keep you warm on a cold day, there's no other form of heating around. How could anyone live in a place like this? There's no bathroom or toilet, just an old sink in the kitchen."

"With the help of a good builder I think it would make a lovely home," said Joan. "It's got character, I bet there are some attractive beams hidden under all those layers of old wall paper."

"I'm not brave enough to tackle anything as bad as this," said Doreen. "There must be somewhere better to live, I'll just have to keep searching."

The estate agents contacted her a few days later and warned her that the prospective buyer for the salon was running out of patience, if she couldn't give him a completion date soon he would look for somewhere else. Reluctantly, she took Jack and Sylvia to see Halford House. They both thought it was wonderful. Sylvia loved the stables and Jack thought there was plenty of room to park cars in the yard, also the top storey of the stone barn would convert into a super pigeon loft.

"Well, if we buy it you're going to have to rough it for a while," Doreen warned. "I hope you're still as keen when you have to use the loo in the yard on a dark cold night and it might be some time before we get a bathroom and hot running water."

Doreen put in a very low offer for the property and it was promptly accepted. She found a builder who could start work straight away. He was enthusiastic about the house and wanted to knock two rooms into one and search for hidden fireplaces but she insisted that his first priority was to sort out the drainage and install main water.

When they moved in she was close to tears. Everything was covered in layers of dust and the furniture packed into two rooms out of the way of the workmen. Even Sylvia was not so keen when she visited the toilet late at night and saw a rat staring at her in the light of her torch.

They had to boil kettles for hot water and wash in the kitchen sink. On the first day as Jack emptied his make do wash basin he watched, intrigued, as the soapy water trickled out through a hole in the wall, ran across the drive and made its way down the lane. It was several weeks before the main water was laid on and the septic tank had been built. One of the bedrooms was to be converted to a luxury bathroom, so Doreen and Joan drove to Bristol to find a firm that specialized in coloured bathroom suites, still quite a rarity, and chose a stylish one in turquoise. When it was finally installed Doreen, Jack and Sylvia took it in turns to have a long hot soak and in future would never take the luxury of modern plumbing for granted.

Louie offered to look after Spot the spaniel while the West household was in such turmoil. Doreen had delivered him to Wayside a couple of days before their move and when they unloaded his blanket, basket, favourite toys and a supply of dog food, she couldn't help smiling. "He's like a small child going on his holidays."

He would probably have got under the feet of the workmen and, as he had a tendency to wander, he might have got lost in the unfamiliar surroundings. He was a bossy little character and Louie enjoyed his company. On the first morning of his vacation he ran into the paddock to chase the ducks and scattered the chickens in all directions, but when he made towards the geese he had his come-uppance. The gander hissed, lowered his head and charged, pecking him sharply on the backside. Louie roared with laughter as she watched the antics. The little dog ran for his life and never pestered her poultry again.

Doreen had told her not to spoil him. "The weather's not cold. He can sleep in the shed." But after spending the evening with him snuggled up on the settee, Louie hadn't the heart to shut him outside so carried his basket into her bedroom. *We'll be company for each other*, she thought.

A week went by and she had been sleeping very well, the little dog never stirred in his bed and she found it comforting to know that he was there. Then one night she awoke with a start and realized that Spot was standing by the door growling. She could hear scuffling and tapping noises coming from outside, someone was obviously trying to break in. She jumped out of bed and grabbed a torch. As she opened her bedroom door Spot ran ahead of her and barked furiously. She hurried to the

221

lounge and peered through the window. When her eyes became accustomed to the darkness she spotted the figure of a man running away across the lawn as fast as his legs would carry him. She turned on all the lights and had a look around but nothing seemed to be missing or damaged so she decided to have a hot drink and go back to bed. *I expect it was just a tramp*, she thought. *It's not worth bothering the police tonight. I'll telephone them in the morning.*

A young police constable arrived the next day soon after Louie's call and together they searched outside the bungalow for any trace of the would-be intruder. Sure enough, there were foot prints in the flower border by the lounge and the window frame was damaged, obviously an attempt had been made to force it open.

"It looks as if someone was up to no good, probably a burglar. It's a good thing your dog frightened him off, Mrs Hutt. It could have been nasty if you'd found him indoors." The policeman sounded quite concerned.

"Actually, he's not my dog, he belongs to my daughter," said Louie. "He's only here for a short stay while she's moving house. He's a wonderful little guard, from the sound of his bark the intruder must have thought he was very big and very fierce. No wonder he ran away so fast."

"Well, I would advise you to get a guard dog of your own if you're living here alone. In the meantime, don't worry. This particular thief is not going to return in a hurry after the fright he's had." After a quick cup of tea the constable was on his way and Louie telephoned Doreen to tell her what had happened.

222

"I'm just thankful Spot was here to protect me," she said. "He was a brave little hero, I'll miss him when he goes. Perhaps I'll buy an Alsatian."

"You keep Spot as long as you like," said Doreen. "I worry about you living at Wayside on your own. Are you still happy there?"

"I love it here." Louie laughed. "It's going to take more than an old tramp to drive me away from my lovely home."

About a week later, Olive woke in the night with a severe headache and crept quietly past Jane's room and down the stairs to get some aspirin from a cupboard in the dining room. When she turned on the light she had the shock of her life. A man was standing with his back to her, apparently looking in the sideboard where her silver was kept. As he swung round she recognized him.

"Freddie Frost!" she shrieked. "What are you doing in my house!" She grabbed hold of an ornamental sabre which was hanging on the wall and waved it in his face until he backed away and stood pinned against a bookcase. She shouted as loudly as she could to wake Jane who rushed down the stairs and telephoned the police. "Fetch the hockey stick from the hall stand, Jane. We're not going to let him get away!"

The two women stood over their captive daring him to move. "What's in that bag?" Olive roared, pointing to a holdall by his feet. When they searched it they found several pieces of her best silverware and a small clock that she was particularly fond of, also some jewellery that they had not seen before.

"We're not the first people that you've robbed tonight are we? How could you do such a spiteful thing when we tried to help you?" Olive was furious. "You told us you were in the antiques business."

"I do deal with antiques," said Freddie. "They just happen to be other people's. There's no need to take it personally, I don't mean you any harm. Stealing is my job. I'll take any valuables I can lay my hands on even if they belong to people I know. You've got plenty of money and I expect you're insured, you could have claimed for any loss."

"No insurance claim could ever replace Olive's family treasures and we have to work very hard to earn a living," said Jane. "How dare you think you can just help yourself to other people's property. I hope you haven't been stealing from any of our friends."

"I did pay a visit to Mrs Hutt last week but her damn dog started barking before I could get in so I had to get away. I was a bit annoyed because she'd got some good stuff and when we went there for tea I didn't see any dogs. I hate the things, they just mean trouble for people like me."

The police arrived and the sergeant recognized Freddie straight away. "Freddie Fingers Frost! We haven't seen you for a while. Have you been on holiday?" he joked.

The little man seemed quite put out. "It's no laughing matter. I've been in hospital, very ill."

"Oh, what a shame," said the policeman. "If I'd known I'd have sent you some flowers. You've obviously made a good recovery as I see you're back to work. Though it looks as if you've met your match with these two brave ladies."

They took him away and Olive and Jane had to give formal statements the next day. The police assured them that there was enough evidence to send Freddie back to prison for some time.

Olive telephoned Louie to tell her what had happened. "I feel so guilty that I brought that dreadful man into your house. You'll never want to see us or our friends again."

"Don't be silly," Louie laughed. "I was taken in by him too, I thought he was charming and even showed him my gold coins. I shall be really hurt if you don't visit any more, I love to see you all. We're not going to let him spoil our fun. I expect he thought that we're a bunch of silly women and stealing from us would be easy. I'm so glad you didn't let him get away with it, but it must have been a frightening experience."

"When I realized who he was, I was too angry to be scared," said Olive. "It was his attitude that annoyed me more than anything, he seemed to think that he had a right to take our things. Ungrateful little crook!"

Elliston and Cavell was the largest department store in Oxford, well known for its quality commodities especially stylish ladies' fashions. Among its many services it boasted a hairdressing salon and a smart restaurant with an excellent lunch-time menu. It was a popular rendezvous for ladies to meet after a morning's shopping, where they could sit and relax and catch up on the latest gossip over a nice meal.

Occasionally, Louie would treat herself to a day in Oxford. Well turned-out in her best suit and hat, she would wander around the shops for a while, then have her hair styled before joining her friends for lunch. After spending much of her time wearing muddy old wellingtons to tend her poultry and clean out chicken houses, it made a pleasant change to feel like an Oxford lady again, not that she hankered to return to the town to live.

Usually, Doreen drove her into the city centre. They would then go their separate ways to save time with their shopping before meeting in the restaurant at one o'clock. On Thursdays they were joined by Olive and Jane as it was early closing day in Oxford and they did not have to work in the afternoons. They liked to drive Louie home to Wayside later for a cup of tea.

Doreen had made arrangements to spend a day in Oxford with Louie, but Sylvia's pony was taken ill and she had to cancel. Louie had been looking forward to her outing for a month and was very disappointed. *I've a good mind to hitchhike into town,* she thought. *Otherwise, I'll have to cancel my appointment with the hairdresser.*

There was now so much noisy traffic on the road by the entrance to Wayside that she could even hear the drone of it indoors. Many of the lorries were car transporters delivering Morris cars from the Cowley works. The Morris Minor had proved so popular that the factory was at full stretch to supply the demand. Louie walked to the lay-by where an empty transporter was parked. The driver and his mate were having a break before returning to the works for another load of cars. They said she was welcome to a lift and took her to the outskirts of Oxford where she was able to catch a bus into the town centre.

She had plenty of time to shop and spent an hour in the hairdressing salon. As she made her way to the restaurant she was feeling relaxed and well-groomed.

"My word. You look smart, Louie," said Joan who was already seated with Olive and Jane at the table. "Doreen told me she'd had to let you down so we weren't expecting to see you today. I'd have offered to drive you but my car is being serviced so I travelled in by bus."

"I don't always have to rely on Doreen," Louie was quite indignant. "I can manage to get around without her."

"The trouble is, Jane and I have dental appointments this afternoon so we shan't be able to drive you home," said Olive.

"That's no problem, I've already made arrangements. Now, what's on the menu today?" said Louie, eager not to dwell on the subject.

They all enjoyed a superb meal attended by smart waitresses in black dresses and white aprons. The four ladies kissed each other goodbye and went their separate ways and it was then that Louie realized she didn't know how she was going to get home. *I suppose I should go by taxi,* she thought, *but it does seem a waste of money if I can get a lift for free.*

She took a bus ride back to where the traffic left a large roundabout on the way to Witney as she remembered having seen other hitchhikers waiting there.

After a short wait a large empty flatbed lorry pulled alongside and she climbed in. The driver told her he was on his way home to Wales after delivering goods to London. He had a rather sullen manner but Louie thought he was probably very tired after such a long journey. The lorry gained speed and seemed to be swerving erratically, sometimes nudging the kerb and then crossing very close to the path of oncoming traffic. The driver swore as he crashed the gears and it was then that Louie realized he was drunk. An empty whiskey bottle was rolling around on the floor of the cab.

Her heart was pounding as she recalled similar unpleasant journeys in Algy's car due to his bad temper and impatience. On one occasion he actually crushed Doreen against a post when she was struggling to open a gate for him.

When they were within half a mile of Wayside, Louie asked the driver if he would stop and let her out but he took no notice of her. "Please will you let me out!" she cried out again. With his foot hard down on the accelerator the driver stared straight ahead, and as they sped past her home she was petrified. After about a mile the lorry suddenly veered across the road, turned into a transport café and skidded to a halt in the large parking area sending up a spray of gravel.

"I thought you'd like to buy me a cup of tea," the driver's speech was slurred.

"Yes of course, I'd be glad to," said Louie as she searched in her handbag for some cash. She grabbed her shopping and almost fell out of the cab in her haste. As the driver was closing his door she thrust a pound note into his hand and then scuttled away. She reached the main road, headed towards home and then it started to pour with rain. She was gasping for breath and her legs felt like lead weights as she hurried along. Every now and then she couldn't help glancing over her shoulder to make sure she wasn't being followed though she knew it was unlikely.

By the time she reached Wayside it was nearly dark. Her suit and hat were wet through, her best shoes caked with mud and her smart hairdo ruined. She had no time to feel sorry for herself as her poultry had to be attended to. When, at last, she had finished all her chores she had a long hot soak in the bath, lit the fire and collapsed onto the settee with a hot drink. Spot nestled close to her. She became aware that she was shaking when she slopped her mug of cocoa as she tried to lift it to her lips, so she gulped down some brandy to steady her nerves. It was not long before the large dose of medicinal alcohol had worked wonders, she felt so much better that she started to giggle. *What an idiot I've been*, she thought. *Going through an ordeal like that just to save the price of a taxi fare. Well I've learnt my lesson the hard way, I shall never risk going hitchhiking again. Worst of all, I've ruined all my best clothes.*

Louie never told anyone what had happened and, for a while, she lost her enthusiasm for shopping trips. Perhaps I'm getting old, she thought, after turning down an invitation from Doreen for a day out. She had told her that she had a cold but really she preferred to stay at home, mess about in the garden and watch her newly hatched chicks running around in the brooder.

229

* * *

On a cold damp November morning, Wilf telephoned
Louie to tell her that he was the proud father of a lovely
little baby girl, who was to be called Valerie, and that
Rosemary was fine.

When Doreen offered to drive her to the hospital to
see her new grandchild, Louie was as keen as mustard,
her frightening experience almost forgotten.

CHAPTER
TWENTY-TWO

By early spring most of the inside improvements had been completed on Halford House and Doreen was very proud of it. The builder had done an excellent job and had proved Joan's prediction to be correct when he stripped the walls in the large sitting room to reveal old oak beams and original stone fireplaces.

Now, Doreen thought she had better start work on the overgrown vegetable garden. It was sheltered on two sides by a high wall which separated it from the neighbouring farmyard. On the other side of a boundary hedge that ran along the bottom was a large house in several acres of grounds which included formal gardens, orchard, vegetables and a lake.

Wilf had recently bought a second-hand mechanical rotovator in a farm sale, so he offered to spend a day giving Doreen a hand. They unloaded the heavy machine from his pick-up truck and dragged it down to the garden where he pulled the starting handle to start the engine. He pulled and pulled, but there was not so much as a splutter. It took him over an hour to find the fault and then the engine started with a deafening roar.

"Never mind, at least it's running," shouted Wilf. "Now we can get to work." As he put it into gear it trundled off turning sods of soil as it went. Wilf gave a "thumbs up" sign and all was well until he reached the end of the row and tried to turn it but to no avail and it hit the garden wall with a crash. Eventually, he manoeuvred it round and headed back towards Doreen who stepped back well out of his way. "I think I'm getting the hang of it," he called out as he plodded past.

He soon mastered the wayward machine and it rapidly cleared a large patch of the neglected garden. Doreen was eager to have a go with the digging so Wilf reluctantly let her take over for a while and it was not long before she was effortlessly sailing up and down in long straight lines, much to his annoyance. However, as she turned the corner at the far end, she lost her balance and it seized its opportunity and ran into the hedge, becoming completely entangled in the branches and stalling the engine. Doreen cursed as she picked herself up and then spotted someone peering through the fence.

"Hello, I'm Frank. I do the gardening here," he said. "I heard a commotion and wondered if you were all right."

"It's nice to meet you, Frank. I'm Doreen," she said. "We're fine, thank you. My brother, Wilf, is helping me to clear the vegetable garden."

"Well, it's nice to see someone taking an interest in the old place again. I'll let you get on, but if you need any help just give me a shout."

As the months went by the vegetables flourished and Doreen would often see Frank for a little chat over the fence. She learnt that he was a bachelor and lived with his brother, Josh, on a small farm where they kept pigs.

He loved his animals and was always keen to tell her about his latest litter.

"I have a great life," he told her one day. "When I'm not in this lovely garden, I'm with my dear old pigs."

Doreen couldn't help noticing that he always wore the same shabby cap in all weathers. "It keeps my head warm," he would say, "and I tucks my money in it. Safer than my trouser pockets 'cos they tend to get a bit holey."

While Jack was at work and Sylvia at school there was nothing Doreen enjoyed more than to spend an hour or two working in the peaceful garden. However, lately she had had an unwelcome visitor who tested her patience to the limits. A large hen from the neighbouring farmyard took great pleasure in flying over the high garden wall and would then set about scratching up seeds and seedlings and generally destroying anything that lay in her path. Doreen would shoo her and chase her away only to find that she had returned the next day.

"If she keeps doing this," she told Joan, "I shall catch her and roast her for dinner."

A few weeks later Joan and Percy were invited to a meal of roast chicken at Halford House.

"By the way, what happened to that tiresome hen that kept ruining your garden?" Percy asked casually.

"Oh I've dealt with her," said Doreen with a wink. "She won't bother me again."

Her guests carried on eating, but rather tentatively. "You needn't worry," she laughed. "I caught her, clipped her wings so that she couldn't fly so high and sent her home. She hasn't been back so it seems to have done the trick."

There was a sigh of relief all round, everyone tucked in to their delicious meal and Percy and Jack could not resist Doreen's offer of a second helping.

Louie was reading her local newspaper one afternoon, while she snatched a quick cup of tea. She noticed a short article about public transport which contained excellent news. There was to be an improved bus service in her area and they would be stopping frequently throughout the day only a stone's throw from her gateway. She had been wondering whether she should spend some of her hard earned savings to buy a little car and take up driving again but now she would be able to hop on a bus and travel to Oxford or Witney whenever she liked. She was so pleased that she set about her afternoon chores with gusto. She was cleaning some windows when she saw a young lad cycling up the drive.

"I've come to buy some eggs for my mum," he said. "She'd like a dozen hen eggs and half a dozen duck eggs."

"You'd better come with me to the store and we'll pop some into a box so that they don't get broken bumping around on your bike. Have you got far to go?"

"Not far, I live in Cassington. It only took me about ten minutes to get here." He seemed reluctant to go. "I wondered if I could have a look at your ducks? My granddad used to keep them on his smallholding and I helped him look after them till he died. He had Aylesburys, Indian Runners and Muscovys and all sorts of bantams. I'd like to keep some bantams but our garden's too small."

Louie showed him around the pens of chickens and ducks and his eyes lit up when he saw the geese. The gander hissed at him but he only laughed. "I love geese, they're my favourites. Can I come and see them again, Mrs Hutt? I'd be glad to give you a hand, I don't mind hard work, I'll do anything. I get bored at home."

"You're welcome to come again whenever you like," said Louie, she had rather taken to the boy and guessed he would be about fourteen years old. "But make sure your mother doesn't mind you coming."

"Oh she won't mind," he said as he picked up his bicycle. "Thank you very much for showing me around, Mrs Hutt. My name's Pete by the way." He carefully placed the eggs in a bag on his handlebars and pedalled off down the drive.

He became a frequent visitor to Wayside and was soon helping Louie with all the outside chores. He was a cheerful lad and she enjoyed his company. His grandfather had obviously taught him well as he seemed knowledgeable in most aspects of poultry keeping.

"If you're going to be my right-hand man I think it's time I gave you some pocket money," said Louie. "I don't expect you to do all this work for nothing."

"I don't want paying. I love coming here," said Pete, but when Louie gave him his first payment he proudly tucked it into his pocket. "I'll save it up for a birthday present for my mum."

Pete's mother, Sandra, came to see Louie, one day. "I hope Pete's not being a nuisance, Mrs Hutt. He spends so much time with you I was afraid you might be fed up with him."

"On the contrary, he's a great help to me," said Louie. "I was worried that you might prefer him to be at home and I wouldn't want him to neglect his homework."

"There's not much for him to do at home and he loves being out with the poultry so, as long as you don't mind him coming, I'm happy." Sandra laughed. "Give him any dirty old job, it'll do him good."

Pete loved to take Spot for a run and was very distressed one afternoon, when he couldn't find him and was told by Louie that he had gone.

"I thought it was time Spot went back to his real home. I shouldn't have kept him away from his family for so long," she said. "I hope you don't mind but I've bought a puppy and I'm afraid I shall need your help to look after him. He's called Jimmy."

She had thought for some time that she ought to buy a young dog as a potential guard but knew that puppies can be hard work. With Pete's help, however, she decided to go ahead and when she showed him the young Alsation he was obviously overjoyed. They were to become the best of friends and as he grew older Jimmy loved to romp and play with the young lad before settling down with Louie in the evenings, always on his best behaviour in the company of a lady.

It was a glorious hot summer and Louie's garden was aglow with colour. Every plant was thriving and she thought it must be due to the vast amounts of chicken manure that Pete had helped her deposit around the borders. As she busied herself amongst the vegetables she was thinking how lucky she was to be fit enough to do the jobs she enjoyed and that all seemed to be well with her family, especially Evelyn and Don who had recently told her that they were expecting their first child. Her only slight worry was that she had not heard from Henry lately.

As she was putting her tools away she noticed a smart little red sports car coming up the drive. The hood was down and as it drew near she thought the driver looked familiar. As he stepped out of the car with a beaming smile, Louie's heart missed a beat.

"Henry! Whatever are you doing here?"

"You've told me so much about Wayside in your letters I thought I'd better come all the way from Singapore just to have a look," he joked. "How are you, Louie?"

"I'm fine, but why didn't you let me know you were coming to England?" She was still trying to come to terms with the shock of seeing him again.

"I wrote to you, didn't you get my letter?" he said. "I shall be staying over here for about a month while I sort out all my affairs, then I shall be going back to Singapore for good."

They spent the rest of the afternoon together chatting and when Louie showed him around her poultry enterprise he seemed intrigued.

"I can see why you're so happy here, but you mustn't work too hard," he said. "This'll be my last chance to see the English countryside so I've bought this little car to travel around. I've always wanted to own a sports car and I shall take it back home to Singapore when I go. I was hoping you might come on a few trips with me?"

"Oh, I don't know," Louie hesitated and then made up her mind. "Yes, I'd love to."

Henry's face lit up. "I'll be in touch in a few days after I've seen my solicitors. If you need to contact me in the meantime, I'm staying at The Randolph Hotel."

"My goodness, that's a bit expensive isn't it?" Louie exclaimed.

"I'm not short of a bob or two," he laughed. "I thought I'd make my last visit to England a memorable one. You must have dinner with me one evening, the food there is quite good." He revved the sporty engine of his car and sped off down the drive.

Two or three times a week, Henry and Louie set out on day trips around the countryside. It was harvest time and the atmosphere was hot and dusty, but with the hood down they were refreshed by a constant cool breeze. They visited Henry's nephew in Wiltshire and spent a couple of days by the sea. They decided to devote one day to visiting some of the Oxford colleges and museums and also found time for a delicious lunch in The Mitre Hotel. A walk through Christchurch meadows and the Botanical Gardens rounded off a perfect day.

Henry was adamant that the destination of their next trip was to be Louie's choice, so they headed off in the direction of Faringdon. They stopped at Kilminsters Farm where Louie had spent the early years of her married life and then on to the heronry, one of her favourite places and where Algy proposed to her. She used to go walking there when she wanted a little time on her own away from the hectic demands of the farm. So many memories came flooding back. Henry thought

238

it was a slightly strange but very beautiful spot as they sat quietly watching the rather weird birds standing on one leg in the water waiting to dab at their prey. The young birds had long since left their untidy nests high up in the trees and were quite active, flying around and tussling with each other for morsels of food.

Louie gave a sigh. "Time to move on," she said. "If we stop here any longer I shall probably burst into tears. Let's go to Burford. My children used to attend the Grammar School but I don't think I've been there since. I wonder if it's changed?"

They parked the car in the pretty Cotswold town and walked down the steep hill to the watch the river Windrush flowing under the bridge. The town had changed, there was more traffic and more busy shops. Louie remembered when cars were few and far between. As they puffed their way back up the hill they stopped to buy fruit and sandwiches.

"I know somewhere quiet where we can eat this," she said. It only took them a few minutes to drive to Minster Lovell where they sat by the river in the grounds of the old ruined manor house and enjoyed their picnic.

They drove on to Carterton and stopped outside the café that Louie ran with the help of Janet and Doreen when they were in their late teens.

"Those girls used to get up to some pranks," she laughed. "They tied up one of the customers when he was misbehaving and I know Doreen used to drive my cake delivery van like a racing car. They met plenty of boy friends in the café, most of our regulars were air force boys from the air base at Brize Norton. They were such lovely chaps, always full of fun, but they must have been very brave, so many were killed flying sorties in that dreadful war."

When they arrived back at Wayside they could see Pete romping with Jimmy in the paddock. "I've fed the hens and collected the eggs, Mrs Hutt," he shouted.

"He's a smashing lad, Louie," said Henry. "Do you think he'd like a day out? We could take Sylvia too. You find out where they'd like to go and we'll arrange something."

"That's a lovely idea. I'm sure they'd enjoy an outing," she said. "I've had a wonderful day today. Thank you for letting me visit some of my old haunts and reminisce."

Pete and Sylvia chose to go to London to visit Madame Tussaud's wax museum. They made an early start on Saturday morning, leaving Jimmy with Doreen in case they were late back. Henry seemed to know his way around London and parked the car in an alleyway not far from the museum. They were all fascinated by the lifelike wax figures, so many celebrities past and present from glamorous film stars to politicians. Then they came to the eerie Chamber of Horrors and Henry gave Louie a nudge and pointed to Pete and Sylvia who were totally engrossed in the macabre scenes. "Look at their faces, they've gone quite white. They probably won't sleep tonight."

"Never mind," laughed Louie. "Shocking it may be, but they're loving every minute."

When they finally emerged into the daylight from the dim lighting in the museum they were feeling hungry so

240

Henry suggested they make their way to Lyons Corner House in The Strand for lunch. The smart, efficient waitresses, popularly known as "nippies", soon served them with tomato soup with crusty rolls and huge portions of fish and chips and still, somehow, they each managed to round off the meal with a Knickerbocker Glory. Louie smiled when she noticed that Sylvia and Pete had raspberry sauce on their chins and there was a smudge of tomato soup on Henry's smart tie. She found herself giving her face an extra dab with the serviette just in case she too was displaying a token of how much she had enjoyed her meal.

"Where shall we go now?" asked Henry. "What about London Zoo?"

There was an enthusiastic chorus of "Yes please!" and it was not long before Sylvia and Pete were happily wandering around with the other visitors gazing at the exotic animals while Louie and Henry found a convenient bench where they could rest their legs. There were hoots of laughter coming from the direction of the monkey enclosure as they put on a show of comical antics, to the delight of their audience.

"I used to come here with Mildred when we were young," said Henry. "She loved animals, especially the monkeys, they made her giggle. In fact, most things made her giggle. I think that's why I fell in love with her, she had such a sense of humour. She'd laugh and say she'd like a job working in the monkey house. It's funny how people change, she used to be such a down to earth girl. I was a student when I met her and she was a cashier in a haberdashery. We had such fun together, I don't know why she became so strait-laced. I expect it was my fault. I don't think anything I did was ever good enough for her."

"Surely not," said Louie. "She had a grand life with you and I'm sure she enjoyed her time abroad."

Just then, the two youngsters appeared, obviously weary. "We can't go another step," gasped Sylvia as they collapsed onto the grass.

Henry laughed. "Then it's time to head for home."

The day before Henry was due to leave for Singapore, he spent the day with Louie at Wayside. They pottered in the garden, collected eggs and sat in the late summer sunshine.

"I expect you're looking forward to going home," she said. "I am, but I shall miss you, Louie. I've grown so fond of you." He hesitated for a moment and seemed to summon up courage before carrying on. "I wondered if there was a chance that you would ever consider marrying me? I'd do my best to make you happy and it's a great life in Singapore. We would have no money worries and I'd make sure you never had to work again. I have a comfortable home and the weather is so warm. No more cold English winters!"

Louie was astounded by Henry's offer. "I don't know what to say! At my age I never expected to get a proposal of marriage. I'm very flattered, but I'm a grandmother and I've been independent for so long I don't think I'd make a very good wife. I do care for you but it would be difficult for me to leave my family and live in a strange country. My roots are here."

"I was afraid I'd be asking too much," said Henry, "but I shan't give up hope that you might change your mind. Will you, at least, come for a holiday?"

"A holiday would be nice," said Louie, but when they later kissed goodbye she was afraid that, sadly, she would probably never see him again.

CHAPTER
TWENTY-THREE

The formerly derelict yard at Halford House was now in full use. Jack's pigeons had settled down well in their new loft and he was able to stay at home on race days. He would sometimes work on his own car in the large garage, nipping out now and then to watch for a homecoming bird.

Doreen and Sylvia had added an extra pony to their string so the stables were fully occupied. They rented a paddock nearby for grazing and there were plenty of outbuildings to store tack and fodder.

One of Jack's favourite magazines was *The Exchange and Mart* and in his spare time he would search the columns for bargains. "There's a young donkey for sale for only seven pounds," he said to Doreen one day. "It sounds very cheap. I wouldn't mind buying it if you'd pay for the delivery."

Sylvia overheard the conversation and set her heart on it straight away. "Please can we have it? I'm sure it wouldn't be any trouble and a little thing like that can't eat much."

Doreen didn't take much persuading and arrangements were made for the little donkey to be delivered the next day. Sylvia hurried home from school just in time to see a large horsebox arrive. They peered inside to see a tiny, bedraggled creature cowering in a corner. It had to be supported down the ramp on its wobbly legs. While Sylvia led it to its snug new home under the pigeon loft, Doreen paid the driver and found to her cost that the delivery charge came to more than the price of the donkey.

There was a catchy song frequently played on the radio at that time called Bimbo, so they christened him Bimbo, though Louie always insistently referred to him as Bingo. When he had recovered from his journey and eaten his fill, Sylvia and Diana groomed him till his coat was clean and fluffy. They stood gazing at him and agreed that they had never seen anything so adorable. Doreen kept returning to his stable to cuddle him and Jack was besotted with him, feeding him titbits at every opportunity. Sylvia's remark that she was sure a little donkey wouldn't be any trouble couldn't have been more wrong. Never had a family enjoyed spending so much time with one small animal, indulging his every whim.

There was a large empty shed in the corner of the yard so Doreen thought it would be nice to keep some hens and have her own fresh eggs. After erecting a wire netting fence to protect her vegetable garden, she bought some Rhode Island Red point-of-lay pullets and waited patiently for the first eggs to appear. Weeks turned to months and she was still waiting. Jack teased her at every opportunity to add to her frustration.

Sylvia let the chickens out one morning and discovered the nest boxes full of eggs. She rushed to tell her mother who proudly gathered them into a basket. Her jubilation, however, was short lived when she realized that they had all been stamped with the sign of a lion.

Another of Jack's pranks, she thought. *I'll make him sorry*.

For the next few days she served him eggs for every meal, boiled, fried, poached, scrambled and served as omelettes.

"Now my hens are laying so well it'll save me buying so much meat," she remarked. "They're lovely eggs, nicer than the bought ones." But she soon forgave him and cooked his favourite roast joint for Sunday lunch. In their own good time the pullets started to lay and their large dark brown eggs were worth waiting for.

Doreen had told Frank about her reluctant layers. "You can't rush 'em, Gal," he chuckled. "They'll lay when they're ready."

She had been watching out for him for about a week, keen to relate that all was now well with her chickens, but had seen no sign of him. She asked her neighbour, Dan, if he had seen Frank lately.

"Haven't you heard?" he said. "I thought everyone knew. He was found dead in the lake on Wednesday. His brother told me that the police think it was suicide."

Doreen was horrified. "Frank wouldn't commit suicide. He was the happiest man I ever knew."

"It seemed strange to me," said Dan. "What puzzles Josh is the fact that they've never found his cap, though they searched all the gardens and the lake. He'd sold some pigs the day before and I bet he had some money stuffed in it."

246

Doreen was saddened over Frank's death. She was going to miss his happy face peering over the fence. Such a kind, gentle man couldn't have had an enemy in the world. Weeks later the coroner's verdict was published in the local paper: Death by misadventure. She was never convinced and felt that there were many questions left unanswered.

Doreen sensed that Louie was feeling rather low and thought she was probably missing Olive and Jane who were away on holiday. It was all the rage to go driving on the Continent and they had saved for the past year to spend a fortnight touring France. They sent Louie a postcard to say that they were having the time of their lives and, as yet, had only got lost twice.

Pete's birthday was only a week away and Louie thought she would give him some bantams and let him keep them in a spare pen in her orchard. Doreen found an advertisement for some Silky bantams for sale on a farm near Abingdon and suggested that they take a drive out to see them and on the way they could call in on Janet.

By the time they reached The Pied Piper it was lunch time and the restaurant was extremely busy. Doreen noticed, with amusement, that most of the diners were smartly dressed business men, each sitting at their own separate tables. Janet was busily helping the waitresses but spotted Doreen and Louie and invited them through to the kitchen.

"I think we've come at a bad time," said Louie. "We didn't expect you to be so busy."

"I added a cheap business lunch to the menu about a month ago," said Janet. "I serve a three course meal for five shillings and now word's got around we're rushed off our feet. We have quite a few regular customers, I think they appreciate a nice hot meal in the middle of the day."

"Now they've tasted your cooking there'll be no getting rid of them," said Doreen. "Isn't there an eligible bachelor or two amongst them? It's time you met someone nice."

"I know Janet's got some admirers," one of the waitresses butted in. "When I'm serving them they keep asking me, 'How is Mrs Ross today?' or 'Shall we be seeing Mrs Ross?' I see their eyes light up when she comes into the dining room."

"Oh, you do talk a load of rubbish, Gilly," Janet pretended to be annoyed. "I've no time for all that. In any case, it would have to be a very special man to take George's place in my heart."

Doreen and Louie were soon on their way in search of bantams and parked the car in the yard at Hilltop Farm. They were welcomed by a jolly little man, his face half-hidden behind a bushy beard.

"I'm Mrs Hutt," said Louie. "We spoke on the phone and you told me you had some nice healthy young Silkys for sale."

"That's right, Madam," he said. "Follow me."

He took them to a pen where some bedraggled bantams were scavenging in the mud. Louie could tell by their scruffy plumage and scaly legs that these were old birds and way past their best.

"Are these the only ones you have for sale?" she asked.

"Yes. You won't find any better than these," he replied.

"Well, I think I'd have a job to find any worse. These birds are neither young nor healthy and you've brought us on a wasted journey! Goodbye Mr Finch." Louie strode off to the car in disgust.

"What sort of an idiot did he think I am?" she said angrily as they drove home.

Doreen burst out laughing. "Well, at least you couldn't call him a barefaced liar."

A few days later they managed to find a genuine breeder and bought six lovely young bantams. When Pete saw them he was overjoyed.

"They're smashing!" he said. "I reckon they're good enough to win in a show. Thank you very much, Mrs Hutt."

In spite of Janet's protestations, she had, in fact, met someone special. Dudley Goffe came into the restaurant for his lunch two or three times a week and it was not long before a casual friendship turned to love. He was a widower and had a teenage daughter called Mary. Having had a distinguished career in the air force, he was now a civil servant working at RAF Abingdon. They became inseparable, spending all their free time together and it was obvious that marriage was on the cards. Six months later a proud Dudley married his "lovely Janet" in St Michael's Church in Oxford.

* * *

After the long hot summer the weather turned more sinister. The autumn was wet and very windy and on the first day of winter severe gales swept across the country. Louie's chimney was damaged, the roof of one of her chicken houses was lifted clean off and two of her favourite trees were uprooted. She was very downhearted but Pete soon arrived to cheer her up.

"Come on Mrs Hutt, I'll give you a hand and we'll soon get this lot cleared up. I reckon I can mend the roof on the chicken house and there'll be a lovely lot of logs from those fallen trees. You'll have to get a builder to do the chimney but I don't think it'll be a very big job."

They made good all the damage and still the winter continued to be very wet and very cold. Louie consoled herself that at least she was going to enjoy her Christmas as her family and friends were coming to spend the day with her. She bought a Christmas tree, festooned the rooms with decorations and started to plan a feast for her guests.

Among the first of her Christmas cards to arrive was one from Henry. After the seasonal greetings he had written a note: I AM STILL HOPING YOU WILL CHANGE YOUR MIND. ALL MY LOVE, HENRY. She placed it on the mantelpiece and, for the time being, put it out of her mind.

Christmas day was sunny and bright. Doreen, Jack and Sylvia were the first to arrive, closely followed by Olive and Jane. Rosemary, Wilf, Valerie, Evelyn and Don all came in one car and finally Janet, Dudley and Mary completed the family gathering.

250

The women set about preparing the food while little Valerie sat on her father's lap patiently listening to the men's conversation which inevitably turned to the topic of motor bikes and Mary and Sylvia took Jimmy for a walk.

As they all sat happily chatting over their meal, Louie watched them contentedly. *This is how Christmas should be*, she thought. *All my lovely family together*. Then, Jane left the room to reappear proudly carrying two bottles of Champagne. After popping the corks accompanied by loud cheers, she filled their glasses.

"We brought these back from France and kept them for a special occasion," said Olive. "I would like to propose a toast to our hostess. A wonderful lady and the best friend anyone could have. Let's all raise our glasses and drink to Louie!"

Later in the evening, when her family had gone home, Louie was able to relax and have a quiet conversation with Olive and Jane.

"It's been a hard winter so far," remarked Olive. "The weather's been so bad, I don't know how you've managed? But I suppose that's what makes our English weather so interesting. We wouldn't want it hot and sunny all the time would we?"

Louie gazed thoughtfully across to Henry's Christmas card, prominently displayed on the mantelpiece, "I don't know. Maybe it might not be so bad?"

THE END

ISIS publish a wide range of books in large print, from fiction to biography. A full list of titles is available free of charge from the address below. Alternatively, contact your local library for details of their collection of ISIS large print books.

Details of ISIS complete and unabridged audio books are also available.

Any suggestions for books you would like to see in large print or audio are always welcome.

7 Centremead
Osney Mead
Oxford OX2 0ES
(01865) 250333

NEATH PORT TALBOT LIBRARY
AND INFORMATION SERVICES

1		25		49		73	
2		26		50		74	
3		27		51		75	
4		28		52		76	
5		29		53		77	11/07
6		30	11/09	54		78	
7	4/19	31		55		79	
8		32		56		80	
9		33		57		81	
10	.	34		58		82	
11		35		59		83	
12		36		60		84	
13		37		61		85	
14		38		62		86	
15		39		63		87	
16		40		64		88	
17		41		65		89	
18		42		66		90	
19		43		67		91	
20		44		68		92	
21		45		69		COMMUNITY SERVICES	
22		46		70			
23		47		71		NPT/111	
24		48		72			